Dumplings Cookbook for Beginr

Bring the Asian Flavors of Pot Stickers into Your Home with Tasty and Easy-To-Replicate Recipes

Copyright © 2023

Sarah Roslin

COPYRIGHT & DISCLAIMER: all rights are reserved by law. No part of this book may be reproduced without the authors' written permission. It is expressly forbidden to transmit this book to others, neither in paper or electronic format, neither for money nor free of charge. What is reported in this book is the result of years of studies and accumulated experience. The achievement of the same results is not guaranteed. The reader assumes full responsibility for their choices. The book is exclusively for educational purposes.

TABLE OF CONTENTS

1	INTRODUCTION	3
2	FAQ	9
3	VEGETARIAN DUMPLINGS	12
4	VEGAN DUMPLINGS	30
5	BEEF DUMPLINGS	39
6	PORK DUMPLINGS	53
7	SEAFOOD AND FISH DUMPLINGS	64
8	POULTRY DUMPLINGS	77
9	SWEET DUMPLINGS	89
10	DIPPING SAUCES	97
11	CONCLUSION	102

1 INTRODUCTION

Dumplings are an extensive genre of dishes that comprises of hunks of dough. The dough is commonly made with flour, wheat, buckwheat, starch and potatoes, and then wrapped around various fillings like pork, lamb, beef, fish, tofu, shrimp, vegetables, sweets and fruits. The dumplings can be sweet and savory. The diversity of Methods prepare dumplings found in many cuisines around the World includes different types such as

- Fried
- Baked
- Boiled
- Steamed
- Simmered
- Pan-Fried
- Deep Fried

A traditional Chinese medicine practitioner named "Zhang Zhongjing" invented dumpling about 1800 years ago during the Era of Eastern Han dynasty (25 – 220 AD). He discovered that many people did not have enough food and warm clothes due to which they suffered from frostbitten ears. He stewed lamb meat, added black pepper and some medicines. He then chopped all the materials and filled the small dough wrappers called "Dumpling". He treated the people by boiling these dumplings and adding them to broth. All the people were recovered from frostbitten ear and then celebrated New Year. After this achievement, people started to copy Zhang's recipe for the treatment of cold.

In May 2015, United States of America listed 26th September as the National Dumplings Day. This day is celebrated annually with an extending vogue of dumplings all over the world. Dumplings offer a great flavor and variety whether served as an appetizer or a main course.

1.1 TERMS OF COOKBOOK

TERMS	EXPLANATION
Bao	Bao means 'Bun'. It is a Chinese bun filled with sweet fillings (such as read bean paste and purple yam) and savory filling (such as meat and vegetables).
Char Siu Bao	Traditionally they are Cantonese buns filled with Barbecue pork and then steamed.
Gyoza	These are Chinese dumplings that are fried and steamed. They are filled with pork and vegetables. They are served with a dipping mixture of soy sauce and vinegar.
Jiaozi	These are traditional Chinese dumplings made with flour and water that are filled with meat and vegetables.
Har Gow	These are traditional Cantonese pleated shaped shrimp dumplings. They are smooth and transparent.
Momo	This is a Nepali dish. These are bite-size dumplings stuffed with cabbage and other vegetables. They are steamed and sometimes air fried.
Mandu	These are classic Korean dumplings, filled with pork, ginger, tofu and garlic chives. They are steamed, pan fried and boiled.

TERMS	EXPLANATION
Pot sticker	They are crescent shaped dumplings filled with pork. They are steamed and served with soy sauce.
Shu Mai	A traditional open-faced Chinese dumplings filled with shrimps and ground pork.
Siu Jiao	A fan shaped basic Cantonese water dumplings. They are boiled and served in broth.
Sheng Jian Bao	They are small pan fried buns filled with pork and gelatin that melts into soup cooking.
Xiao Long Bao	A type of soup bun. They are usually filled with meat (traditionally pork) and steamed, then placed in soup.
Wonton	A round shape Chinese cuisine. They are steamed and boiled then served with soup.

1.2 KITCHEN TOOLS NEEDED TO MAKE DUMPLINGS

These basis kitchen tools that are almost available in every hold will make your journey to homemade healthy dumplings a lot easier. The tools you need are:

1. Rolling Pin
2. Fish Spatula
3. A Flat Spatula
4. Spider Strainer
5. Dough Scrapper
6. Bamboo Steamer
7. Non Stick Skillet
8. Digital Food Scale
9. Large Sieve Strainer
10. Rectangular Blade Knife
11. Stainless Steel Steaming Tray
12. Extra-Long Cooking Chopsticks

1.3 MAKING OF BASIC DUMPLING WRAPPERS

In order to make a perfect dumpling dough start by weighing your Ingredients
- All Purpose Flour 7 oz.
- Warm water ³/₄ cup
- Wooden Rolling Pin 11-inch long

Preparation Time: 1 hour 30 minutes | Cooking Time: 0 minutes | Servings: 35

1. The temperature of water should not be very cold or very hot, it should be between 110°F to 130°F or 43°C to 54°C. Dumplings dough made with warm water stays in it's perfect shape. Whereas, the dough made with hot water have no elasticity and the dough made with cold or room temperature water shrinks back while rolling. Make sure all purpose flour and water are in 2:1 ratio.
2. Start by adding all purpose flour and warm water into the bowl and start mixing until all the mixture comes all together.
3. Dig your fingers in a claw like motion and gather all the dough.
4. Then take all the dough out on a surface and start kneading for 2-3 minutes until it becomes a smooth ball.
5. If the dough is sticky pour a small amount of all purpose flour onto the surface and knead again.
6. Then leave the dough for maximum 45 minutes to rest. The longer it rests the easier it rolls out. Cover the dough with silicone lid or wet towel.

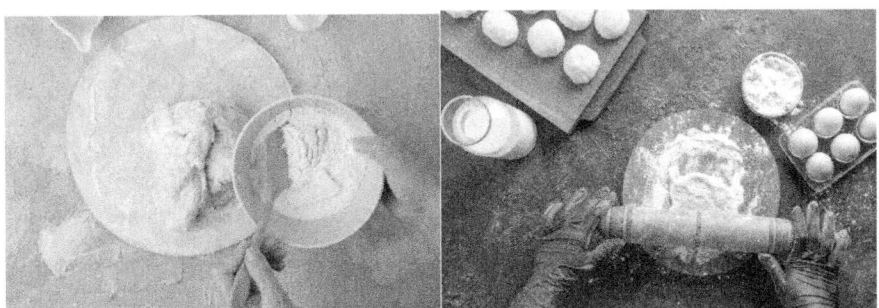

7. Take the dough out and knead again few times.
8. Then make a round ball of the dough and insert a finger in the center of the ball and start rotating it.
9. Roll the dough several times until it makes a big ring of dough that is 1.5 inches in diameter.
10. Cut few pieces of about 2/5 oz. (0.45 oz.) from the rope of dough.
11. Cover the dough again after taking few cuts as it dries out very fast.

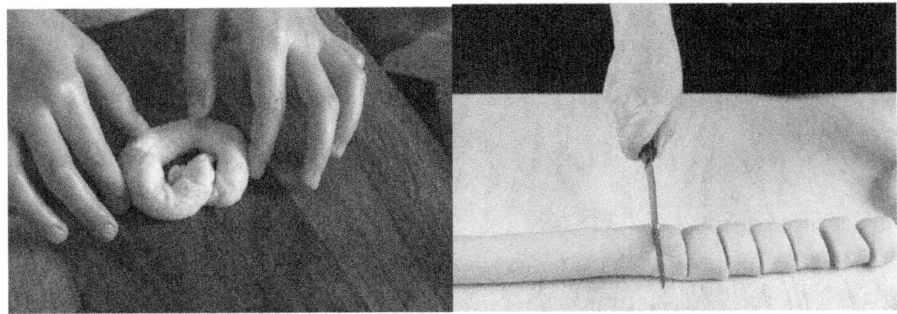

12. Take your wooden rolling pin and start to roll the disc with your right hand. Move the wrapper 90° to left with your left hand and repeat this process 2 times until you get a 3 inches round wrapper. If the wrapper sticks to the rolling pin brush with all purpose flour.
13. Make sure the wrapper is thin at the edges and thick at bottom so the filling does not come out easily.
14. Use can also refrigerate these wrappers for 2 days and freeze them for about a month. For storing these, you need to make a stack of all the wrappers one above the other and brush them with all purpose flour so they do not stick to each other. Wrap this stack tightly with a plastic wrapper and then transfer them into an air tight container.

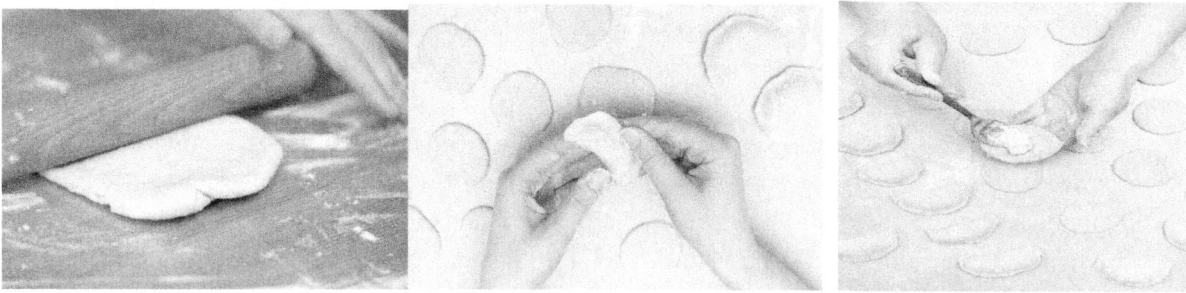

15. The measurements mentioned above will make 35 wrappers each of 3 inches round.

Nutritional Facts / Serving
Carbohydrates: 0.25oz | Protein: 0.032oz | Fat: 0.0035oz | Sodium: 07oz | Fiber: 0.0071oz

1.4 DUMPLING FOLDS

There are various Methods used around the world to folds dumplings. Reference images are added below.

- Rectangular shaped dumplings

- Round wrappers that are folded to form a crescent shape dumpling

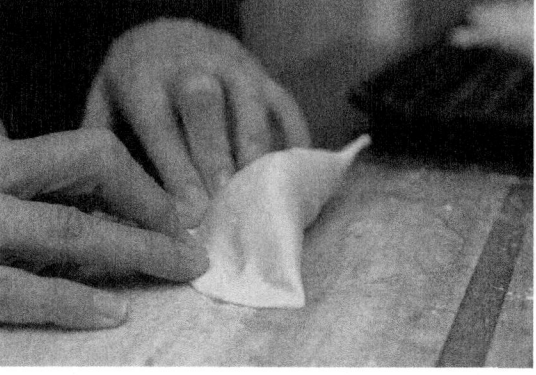

- Open Faced dumplings called "Sui Mai"

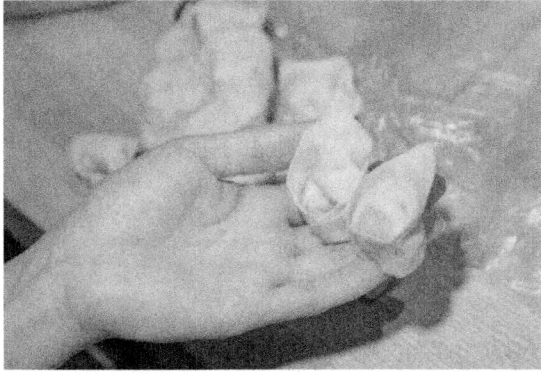

- Classic Korean Mandu
- Pie crust dumplings, usually sweet in nature

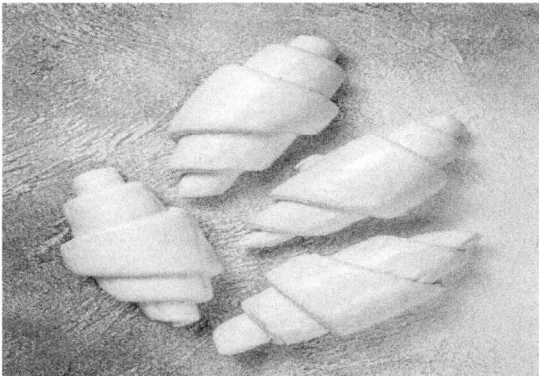

- Rectangular poached dumplings

- Some familiar dumplings seen all around the globe

2 FAQ

Why do dumplings fall apart when cooked?
There are multiple reasons for this failure such as forceful boiling, over cooking, poor sealing technique, excessive use of flours, no use of binders and large chunks found in the filling.

Is gnocchi a kind of pasta or dumpling?
Gnocco means "lump" and gnocchi is a "lump of something". Gnocchi is basically naked dumplings made of dough or a mixture of various Ingredients such as flour, potatoes, herbs and eggs.

My dough is too sticky/ too firm. Any way to fix it?
Add a small amount of flour in your dough and knead it properly until everything comes together. If the dough is too firm knead it with wet hands to keep it hydrated and leaving it for longer period of time will make it softer.

I prefer less chewy wrappers. How can I alter this?
Use warm water for dough or you can also replace your ¼ part of all purpose flour with corn starch.

Can you make semi-transparent, dim-sum style wrappers with this dough?
No, you cannot make dim-sum style because semi-transparent wrappers are made of wheat starch.

Do gluten free wrappers exit?
Yes, you can check gluten free labels of wheat starch to make semi-transparent wrappers.

What kind of rolling pin to use?
To make wrappers, you can use Chinese rolling pin of 1.2 inches in diameter and approximately 11 inches long that has no handles.

Can I make wrappers in different colors?
Yes, different colors can be obtained by adding natural dye Ingredients such as purple cabbage, beetroot, spinach and carrots.

How big the wrappers should be?
The wrappers should be of 3 inches in diameter.

Do I need to cook the filling before assembling?
No, filling goes raw in the dumplings but there are few exceptions like eggs and meat.

Can I leave uncooked dumplings on the counter / in the fridge for few hours?
No, you have to cook them straight away or freeze them.

How to make pan-fried dumplings with a lace like skirt?
For crispy skirt, pan fry the dumplings in starchy slurry instead of water.

How many dumplings make an adult serving size?
The average of around 15 dumplings make an adult serving size.

How to reheat left over boiled dumplings?
Left over dumplings can be pan fried in small amount of oil. They are flipped and heated evenly.

Can you microwave frozen dumplings?
You can pan fry them or put them in bowl with half an inch of water and place the frozen dumpling inside the bowl. Microwave the dumplings for 7-8 minutes.

What's the difference between a dumpling and a pot sticker?
Dumplings and pot sticker belongs to same family. Dumplings are boiled, steamed, fried and smoked. Whereas, pot stickers are pan fried and then small amount of water is added to a closed pan in order to steam them.

What's the difference between a pot sticker dumpling and gyoza?
Both have same appearance, fillings and shape. Pot sticker is a Chinese style pan fried dumplings while Gyoza is a Japanese style pan fried dumplings.

What are pierogis?
These are polished dumplings made out of dough that contains eggs. These are filled with onions, mashed potatoes, mince and cheese. They are boiled and then fried butter until turned crispy. Pierogis are served with some side dish or sauce made of apple.

Can I steam dumplings in a frying pan?
Yes, but it completely depends on the depth of your pan. If your pan has a lid, then you can steam the dumplings by adding water and a steaming rack into your pan. Place the dumplings on the rack and steam them making sure they do not dip in the water.

What side dishes go with dumplings?
Dumplings can be eaten with your choice of side. Most people prefer mushrooms, beef stroganoff and tomatoes as side dishes with dumplings.

How long does it take for dumplings to cook in a stew?
They don't take a long time to cook. It can be checked with a toothpick by putting it in the dumplings, if it comes out clear they are done.

Are Chinese steamed dumplings gluten free?
No, we cannot say they are gluten-free. Because mostly the dough is made with wheat flour. For gluten free dumplings, they should be made with gluten-free flour and for filling use a chestnut powder. A sauce can be only soy based eg; tamari.

Are dumplings healthy?
When eaten in portions along with nutritious sides they are considered healthy.

Can pregnant women have dumplings?
Yes, they can but with careful administration. As chinese food contain high sodium content which can lead to preeclampsia and hypertension. Whereas, Steamed dumplings is the safest option when taken in portion.

Can diabetic people have dumplings?
Yes, they can have but in moderation.

Can people with hypercholesterolemia have dumplings?
Yes, they can have boiled and steamed dumplings. But they should avoid dumplings with meat and pork fillings.

3 VEGETARIAN DUMPLINGS

3.1 Classic Vegetarian Dumplings

Preparation Time: 15 minutes | Cooking Time: 35 minutes | Servings: 30

Ingredients

- Egg - 1
- Mushrooms - 4 oz.
- Bamboo shoots - 2 oz.
- Honey – $1^1/_2$ tsp
- Cabbage - 1 oz.
- Dried Tofu - 1 oz.
- Salt - ½ tsp
- Pepper - ½ tsp
- Sesame Oil - 2 tsp
- Olive Oil - 2 tsp

Preparation

1. Take dry mushrooms and dip them in water for 20-25 minutes. After that drain all the water and cut them in small cubes.
2. Add oils, salt, honey and pepper in a bowl and stir them properly.
3. Wash all the vegetables and cut them into small pieces and squeeze tightly to drain all the liquid.
4. Mix all your vegetables in the oil mixture.
5. In a separate bowl whisk the egg.
6. Take dumpling wrappers and add filling in the center, pinch it to seal.
7. Boil your dumplings for about 5 minutes and serve with dipping sauce of your choice.

Nutritional Facts

Calories: 1398 | Carbohydrates: 14.8g | Protein: 14.1g | Fat: 33.3g | Fiber: 3.1g | Cholesterol: 186mg | Sugar: 3.3g | Sodium: 2345mg

3.2 Pine Nut Gyoza Wraps

Preparation Time: 15 minutes | Cooking Time: 45 minutes | Servings: 28

Ingredients

- Tofu - 110 oz.
- Cilantro - ½ cup
- Ginger - 2tbsp
- Garlic - 1 tsp
- Soy Sauce - 2 tsp
- Sugar - 1 tsp
- Orange Peel - 1 tbsp.
- Pine Nuts - 6 tbsp.
- Mushrooms - 0.5 oz.
- Egg - 1
- Salt - ½ tsp

- Canola Oil - 2 tbsp.

Preparation
1. Squeeze tofu and let all the water to drain.
2. Take a pan and boil your mushrooms for at least 30 minutes and chop them. Save the water for later use.
3. Take a bowl and combine all Ingredients
4. Take your gyoza wraps and filling and seal to make a crescent shape.
5. Take a large pan and add pot stickers and cook for 3-4 minutes until they turn golden brown.
6. Now add leftover mushroom water and let them sizzle for 7-8 minutes. Remove pot stickers with tong and serve them hot.

Nutritional Facts
Calories: 1465 | Carbohydrates: 158g | Protein: 43g | Fat: 78g | Fiber: 16.3g | Cholesterol: 186mg | Sugar: 3.6 | Sodium: 3369mg

3.3 Spinach Stuffed Wontons

Preparation Time: 35 minutes | Cooking Time: 10 minutes | Servings: 50

Ingredients
- Black Mushrooms - 7
- Spinach - ½ lb.
- Carrots - 2 large
- Garlic - 2 cloves
- Soy sauce - 2 tbsp.
- Salt - 1 tsp
- Hoisin Sauce - 2 tbsp.
- Sesame Oil - 1 tbsp.
- Egg - 1
- Wonton Wraps - 50

Preparation
1. Finely chop mushrooms, spinach, carrots and garlic.
2. In a bowl combine egg, soy sauce, salt, hoisin sauce, sesame oil and whisk them.
3. Add vegetables in the mixture.
4. Take wonton wraps put on smooth area.
5. Start filling 1 tbsp. of mixture in a wrap and close them using water around edges.
6. Boil wontons for about 4 minutes and serve them in a nice platter.

Nutritional Facts
Calories: 1398 | Carbohydrates: 131g | Protein: 14.1g | Fat: 28g | Fiber: 5.9g | Cholesterol: 3mg | Sugar: 3.3g | Sodium: 2345mg

3.4 Boiled Chinese Dumplings

Preparation Time: 35 minutes | Cooking Time: 10 minutes | Servings: 30

Ingredients
- Spinach - ½ lb.
- Tofu - 90 oz.
- Mushrooms - 3 oz.
- Chinese Cabbage - 2 oz.
- Garlic - 2 tsp
- Sesame Oil - 2 tsp
- Soy Sauce - 2 tbsp.
- Salt - ½ tsp
- Pepper - ½ tsp

Preparation
1. Boil mushrooms and finely dice them.
2. Crumble tofu and crush garlic in a bowl.
3. Chop Chinese cabbage and add with tofu.
4. Add sesame oil, salt and pepper.
5. Take dumplings wrap and fill them with 1 tbsp. filling. Close them in half-moon shape.
6. Boil for few minutes until they float above the surface.
7. Serve them hot.

Nutritional Facts
Calories: 1140 | Carbohydrates: 127g | Protein: 22g | Fat: 51g | Fiber: 5g | Cholesterol: 2.1mg | Sugar: 3g | Sodium: 2345mg

3.5 Classic Chinese Wontons

Preparation Time: 25 minutes | Cooking Time: 10 minutes | Servings: 30

Ingredients
- Carrots - 2 large
- Spring Onions - 3 tbsp.
- Chinese Cabbage - ½ lb.
- Garlic - 3 cloves
- Ginger - 1 tbsp.
- Sesame Seeds - 1 tsp
- Honey - 1 tsp
- Salt - ½ tsp
- White Pepper - ½ tsp
- Eggs - 2
- Olive Oil - 2 tsp

Preparation
1. Finely chop carrots, spring onions, Chinese cabbage, ginger and garlic.
2. Whisk eggs in a bowl and make scrambles eggs in a nonstick skillet using oil and crumble them.
3. Add eggs and vegetables together and start filling your wontons.
4. Carefully close and seal them.
5. Boil for few minutes until they float on water and dish out in a platter.
6. Serve with chili oil dipping sauce.

Nutritional Facts

Calories: 1243 | Carbohydrates: 113g | Protein: 33g | Fat: 55g | Fiber: 5.5g | Cholesterol: 5mg | Sugar: 3g | Sodium: 1977mg

3.6 Mushrooms and Oyster Sauce Dumplings

Preparation Time: 25 minutes | Cooking Time: 10 minutes | Servings: 30

Ingredients

- Cabbage - ½ lb.
- Salt - ½ tsp
- Mushrooms - ½ cup
- Carrots - 1 large
- White onions - 2 large
- Sesame Oil - 2 tsp
- Soy Sauce - 2 tsp
- Spring Onions - ¼ cup
- Cilantro - ¼ cup
- Oyster Sauce - 2 tbsp.
- White Pepper - ½ tsp
- Canola Oil - 1 tsp

Preparation

1. Add salt to chopped cabbage and set aside.
2. Chop carrots, mushrooms and white onions. Sauté these vegetables in canola oil for 2-3 minutes.
3. Squeeze cabbage and add in sautéed vegetables.
4. Add the remaining Ingredients in the mixture.
5. Take dumpling wrappers, fill with 1 tbsp. of mixture.
6. Shape and seal them accurately, boil for 5 minutes.
7. Serve with red chili sauce.

Nutritional Facts

Calories: 1345 | Carbohydrates: 125g | Protein: 39g | Fat: 69g | Fiber: 5.1g | Cholesterol: 5mg | Sugar: 3g | Sodium: 1990mg

3.7 Cream Cheese Wontons

Preparation Time: 15 minutes | Cooking Time: 10 minutes | Servings: 20

Ingredients

- Vegan Mayonnaise - 3 tbsp.
- Cream Cheese - ½ cup
- Cilantro - ¼ cup
- Spring Onions - 3 tbsp.

Preparation

1. Chop cilantro and spring onions.
2. Mix vegan mayo, cream cheese and cilantro.
3. Take 1 tbsp. of mixture and fill wonton wraps.
4. Boil wontons for 5-7 minutes and served with topped spring onions.

Nutritional Facts

Calories: 740 | Carbohydrates: 30g | Protein: 12g | Fat: 5g | Fiber: 3g |Cholesterol: 1.5mg | Sugar: 2.1g | Sodium: 1373mg

3.8 Stuffed Pea Wontons

Preparation Time: 15 minutes | Cooking Time: 15 minutes | Servings: 25

Ingredients

- White Onions - ½ cup
- Spring Onions - ¼ cup
- Carrots - 2 large
- Capsicum - ¼ cup
- Frozen Peas - ½ cup
- Salt - 1 tsp
- Pepper - ½ tsp
- Soy Sauce - 2 tsp
- Balsamic Vinegar - 2 tsp
- Olive Oil - 2 tbsp.

Preparation

1. Chop all vegetables finely and add them to a large bowl.
2. Add salt, pepper, soy sauce, and balsamic vinegar in the vegetables and mix everything well.
3. Take wonton wraps and place on a clear area and 1 tbsp. of mixture in each wrap and seal it.
4. Pan fry all the wontons in two batches and served them with spicy sauce.

Nutritional Facts

Calories: 937 | Carbohydrates: 45g | Protein: 19g | Fat: 11g | Fiber: 7g |Cholesterol: 1.7mg | Sugar: 3g | Sodium: 2790mg

3.9 Schezwan Veg Bao

Preparation Time: 15 minutes | Cooking Time: 25 minutes | Servings: 30

Ingredients

- Warm Water - ¼ cup
- Sugar - 1 tsp
- Dry Yeast - ½ tsp
- All Purpose Flour - 1 cup
- Salt - ½ tsp
- Oil - 4 tsp
- Onion - 1
- Ginger Garlic Paste - 1 tsp
- Cabbage - 1 cup
- Capsicum - 1
- Soy Sauce - 1 tsp
- Schezwan Sauce - 2 tsp

Preparation

1. Put warm water in a bowl and add sugar and dry yeast. Stir them and keep aside until it becomes double in size.

2. Add all purpose flour in a yeast mix and knead to make a fine dough. If it becomes sticky add 1 tsp of oil and knead again. Keep it aside.
3. On other hand, chop all vegetables and sauté them by adding oil and ginger garlic paste. Put all your seasonings and sauces in it. Mix well.
4. Divide dough into 4 portions and roll each portion into a thick circle and add a good amount of filling inside the center of dough. Seal the dough into round bun.
5. Transfer buns onto parchment paper and steam them for 25 minutes.
6. Soft and fluffy bao buns are ready to serve with any chili sauce.

Nutritional Facts
Calories: 1271 | Carbohydrates: 109g | Protein: 29g | Fat: 35g | Fiber: 15g | Cholesterol: 35mg | Sugar: 3g | Sodium: 2130mg

3.10 Leak and Pea Dumplings

Preparation Time: 15 minutes | Cooking Time: 15 minutes | Servings: 30

Ingredients
- Fresh Ginger - ¼ tsp
- Garlic - 1 tsp
- Sugar - 2 tsp
- Pea Shoots - 1 ¼ lb.
- Dried Mushrooms - 3 cups
- Water - For Boiling
- Canola Oil - 1 tsp
- Chopped Leeks - 3 cups
- Salt - ½ tsp
- Black Pepper - ½ tsp
- Tofu - 6 oz.
- Egg White - 1
- Frozen Pea - ½ cup
- Oyster Sauce - ¼ cup

Preparation
1. Boil water and add salt. Pour pea shoots and boil for 2 minutes. After boiling transfer them quickly to ice water. On other hand, boil mushrooms and dice them.
2. In a pan cook leek, salt and pepper for about 5 minutes.
3. Add pea shoots, tofu and egg. Chop them evenly.
4. Combine tofu mixture, pea shoots, cooked leeks and mushrooms in a large bowl. Pour all your seasonings, sauces, sugar, ginger and garlic.
5. Fill dumplings wrapper and stir fry them in a nonstick skillet for 5-7 minutes.
6. Serve with the choice of your dip.

Nutritional Facts
Calories: 1191 | Carbohydrates: 97g | Protein: 37g | Fat: 21g | Fiber: 19.5g | Cholesterol: 21mg | Sugar: 2.3g | Sodium: 1904mg

3.11 Stir Fry Edamame Wontons

Preparation Time: 25 minutes | Cooking Time: 15 minutes | Servings: 60

Ingredients
- Soy Sauce - 2 tbsp.
- Chili Flakes - ¼ tsp
- Shelled Edamame - 1 lb.
- Lemon - 2
- Salt - ½ tsp
- Ground Pepper - ½ tsp
- Olive Oil - 3 tbsp.
- Wonton Wrappers - 1 lb.

Preparation
1. Divide edamame into 2 portions.
2. Combine soy sauce, edamame, oil and chili flakes. Chop them into a fine paste.
3. Add remaining edamame to chopper and roughly chop them.
4. Combine all the mixture in a large bowl add salt, pepper and squeeze lemons. Mix all Ingredients evenly.
5. Fill wonton wrappers and stir fry them in a skillet on a medium flame for 5 minutes.
6. Serve them hot.

Nutritional Facts
Calories: 1798 | Carbohydrates: 141g | Protein: 38g | Fat: 98g | Fiber: 19g | Cholesterol: 17mg | Sugar: 3.3g | Sodium: 3445mg

3.12 Snow Pea Mint Dumplings

Preparation Time: 25 minutes | Cooking Time: 10 minutes | Servings: 50

Ingredients
- Frozen Peas - 2 cups
- Sliced Snow Pea - 3 cups
- Tofu - 10 oz.
- Sugar - 2 tbsp.
- Canola Oil - 2 tsp
- Fresh Mint (Chopped) - 1 cup
- Lemon Juice - 2 tsp
- Salt - 1 tsp
- Black Pepper - 1 tsp
- Ginger Slice - 2 tsp
- Chopped Scallions - 2 tsp
- Dumpling Wraps - 50

Preparation
1. In a chopper add tofu, frozen pea, sugar and oil. Make a smooth puree.
2. In a large bowl combine all the reaming Ingredients with puree, mix and knead evenly.
3. Fill the dumpling wraps and stir fry them 5 minutes.

4. Serve with any mint sauce.

Nutritional Facts

Calories: 1049 | Carbohydrates: 115g | Protein: 21g | Fat: 75g | Fiber: 15g | Cholesterol: 11mg | Sugar: 2.3g | Sodium: 2906mg

3.13 Kale and Runny Egg Dumplings

Preparation Time: 25 minutes | Cooking Time: 10 minutes | Servings: 30

Ingredients

- Eggs - 4
- Diced Tofu - 8 oz.
- Chopped Kale Leaves - Fresh 1 cup
- Garlic Chives - 2 tbsp.
- Onion Chopped - 1 tbsp.
- Soy Sauce - ½ tsp
- Canola Oil - 1 tsp
- Salt - ½ tsp
- Sugar - ½ tsp
- Sesame Oil - ½ tsp

Preparation

1. In a nonstick pan break 3 eggs and whole white part and keep the yolk runny.
2. In a large bowl combine tofu, kale, chives, onions, soy sauce, salt, sugar, sesame oil and break the remaining 1 egg and mix everything equally.
3. Fill dumplings wrap with 1 tbsp. and seal them.
4. Stir fry in canola oil for 5-7 minutes and serve with ginger dip.

Nutritional Facts

Calories: 1785 | Carbohydrates: 245.3g | Protein: 50.3g | Fat: 94g | Fiber: 9.1g | Cholesterol: 55mg | Sugar: 11g | Sodium: 2051mg

3.14 Pumpkin Squash and Corn Dumplings

Preparation Time: 15 minutes | Cooking Time: 40 minutes | Servings: 45

Ingredients

- Pumpkin Squash - 1lb.
- Minced Onion - 2tsp
- Grated Ginger - 1 tsp
- Fresh Corns - 1 cup
- Cayenne Pepper - 1/8 tsp
- Salt - ½ tsp
- Coconut Oil - ½ tsp
- Brown Sugar - 2 tsp
- Dumpling Wraps - 45

Preparation

1. Steam pumpkin squash for 25 minutes and with the help of spoon scoop out all the squash.
2. Add squash to large bowl and combine with all Ingredients.

3. Fill mixture in the dumpling wraps and stir fry for 7 minutes.
4. Serve them with lemon sauce.

Nutritional Facts
Calories: 2319 | Carbohydrates: 124.8g | Protein: 104.1g | Fat: 93.3g | Fiber: 15.1g | Cholesterol: 98.5mg | Sugar: 55g | Sodium: 3501mg

3.15 Chickpea Wontons

Preparation Time: 15 minutes | Cooking Time: 25 minutes | Servings: 45

Ingredients
- Canned Chickpeas - 15 oz.
- Bell Pepper – Red - 1 cup
- Diced Carrots - ½ cup
- Diced Onion – Red - ¼ cup
- Lemon Juice - ¼ cup
- Salt - ½ tsp
- Canola Oil - 4 tsp
- Sesame Oil - 2 tsp
- Soy Sauce - 2 tsp
- Wonton Wraps - 1lb

Preparation
1. Add canola oil, sesame oil and chickpeas in a chopper and blend them to a smooth paste.
2. Combine chickpea paste along with all vegetables and seasonings.
3. Fill wonton wraps and steam them for 15 – 20 minutes.
4. Serve wontons with lemon and yogurt sauce.

Nutritional Facts
Calories: 2112 | Carbohydrates: 164.4g | Protein: 62.3g | Fat: 45g | Fiber: 11.1g | Cholesterol: 5.5mg | Sugar: 4.1 | Sodium: 3154mg

3.16 Spinach and French Lentil Momos

Preparation Time: 25 minutes | Cooking Time: 37 minutes | Servings: 45

Ingredients
- French Lentils 1/3 cup
- Spinach - 1 lb.
- Salt - ½ tsp
- Water - as needed
- All Purpose Flour - ¼ cup
- Cottage Cheese - 1cup
- Olive Oil - ¼ cup
- Black Pepper - ½ tsp
- Scallions - 3 tbsp.
- Cumin Powder - 1 tbsp.
- Lemon Juice - 1 tsp
- Dumpling Wrappers - 45

Preparation
1. Boil spinach in salt water for about 30 seconds. Drain water and transfer spinach to ice water immediately.
2. Now add French lentils in boiling water and let them simmer for 17 minutes. Drain out excessive water.
3. Sauté flour in oil and add cheese, cumin and spinach. Remove from heat and add lentils, seasonings and lemon juice. Stir all Ingredients to mix equally.
4. Fill mixture in the dumpling wraps and air fry momos for 15-20 minutes on 180°C.
5. Garnish scallions on top and serve with lemon juice.

Nutritional Facts
Calories: 1733 | Carbohydrates: 90g | Protein: 55g | Fat: 14g | Fiber: 13g | Cholesterol: 35mg | Sugar: 9.2 | Sodium: 2212mg

3.17 Cheesy Jalapeno Dumplings

Preparation Time: 15 minutes | Cooking Time: 10 minutes | Servings: 12

Ingredients
- Cream Cheese - ¼ Cup
- Jalapeno Peppers - ¼ Cup
- Milk - 2 tbsp.
- Garlic Powder - 1 tsp
- Cumin - 1 tsp
- Oil - 3 tsp
- Dumpling Wraps - 12

Preparation
1. In a bowl mix all the Ingredients and dropped jalapeno peppers. Mix everything evenly.
2. Spoon-fill Ingredients in dumpling wrappers and seal them.
3. Stir fry for 10 minutes until golden brown.
4. Serve with a sweet and tangy sauce.

Nutritional Facts
Calories: 1113 | Carbohydrates: 62.4g | Protein: 10.3g | Fat: 19g | Fiber: 1.9g | Cholesterol: 4mg | Sugar: 1.6g | Sodium: 1793mg

3.18 Mushroom Packed Wontons

Preparation Time: 25 minutes | Cooking Time: 15 minutes | Servings: 12

Ingredients
- Mushrooms - 1 Cup
- Spring Onions - 3 tbsp.
- Garlic Clove - 1
- Cream Cheese - 4 oz.
- Parmesan Cheese - ¼ Cup
- Salt - ½ tsp
- Pepper - ½ tbsp.
- Cayenne Pepper - 1 tsp
- Oil - 1 Cup

- Bread Crumbs - ¼ Cup
- Worcestershire Sauce - 1 tbsp.
- Wonton Wrapper - 12

Preparation
1. Take a Wok and cook mushrooms, onions, Worcestershire sauce, and garlic. Cook till all the liquid in evaporated.
2. Cool to room temperature and add the remaining Ingredients.
3. Fill wonton wraps and deep fry them until they turn golden.
4. Serve with lemon sauce.

Nutritional Facts
Calories: 3207 | Carbohydrates: 165g | Protein: 45g | Fat: 27g | Fiber: 2.1g | Cholesterol: 14mg | Sugar: 2.1 | Sodium: 3530mg

3.19 Stir Fried Pizza Dumplings

Preparation Time: 25 minutes | Cooking Time: 10 minutes | Servings: 12

Ingredients
- Pizza Sauce - ½ Cup
- Garlic Powder - ½ tbsp
- Italian Seasoning - ½ tbsp
- Salt - ½ tsp
- Pizza Topping (Vegetables of choice) - ½ Cup
- Dumpling Wraps - 12
- Mozzarella Cheese - 1 Cup

Preparation
1. Combine pizza sauce, garlic powder, and Italian seasonings. Bring them to a boil.
2. Add the remaining Ingredients along with all the pizza toppings.
3. Fill dumpling wraps and stir fry them for 5 minutes.
4. Serve with pizza sauce.

Nutritional Facts
Calories: 1434 | Carbohydrates: 103g | Protein: 92g | Fat: 84g | Fiber: 15.1g | Cholesterol: 16.5mg | Sugar: 9.2 | Sodium: 3217mg

3.20 Vegetarian Ricotta Wontons

Preparation Time: 25 minutes | Cooking Time: 10 minutes | Servings: 12

Ingredients
- Mozzarella Cheese - ½ Cup
- Ricotta Cheese - 8 oz.
- Garlic Powder - 1 tsp
- Onion Powder - 1 tsp
- Italian Seasonings - 1 tsp
- Oil - 1 Cup
- Wonton Wrappers - 12

Preparation
1. Mix all the Ingredients and fill in the wonton wrappers.
2. Pour oil into a pan, and heat in medium to high flame.
3. Fry dumplings for 3-5 minutes.
4. Serve with chili sauce.

Nutritional Facts
Calories: 1993 | Carbohydrates: 67g | Protein: 53g | Fat: 27g | Fiber: 8.4g | Cholesterol: 18.5mg | Sugar: | Sodium: 1955mg

3.21 Egg and Soy Dumplings

Preparation Time: 25 minutes | Cooking Time: 10 minutes | Servings: 12

Ingredients
- Egg - 1
- Soy - ¼ Cup
- Cheese Shreds - ¼ Cup
- Onion - ¼ Cup
- Mushrooms - ¼ Cup
- Bell Pepper - ¼ Cup
- Avocado - ¼ Cup
- Oil - 1 tbsp.
- Dumpling Wrappers - 12

Preparation
1. Look vegetables-egg and soy in the same pan. Add cheese on top and mix all Ingredients equally.
2. Fill dumpling wrappers and add mixture. Close and seal them.
3. Stir fry in 1 tbsp. of oil and serve hot with salsa sauce.

Nutritional Facts
Calories: 1140 | Carbohydrates: 149g | Protein: 60.2g | Fat: 18g | Fiber: 5.2g | Cholesterol: 20.1mg | Sugar: 5.3g | Sodium: 3029mg

3.22 Tofu Salad Dumplings

Preparation Time: 35 minutes | Cooking Time: 15 minutes | Servings: 12

Ingredients
- Crumbled Tofu - 1 Cup
- Pickle Relish - 1tbsp.
- Mayonnaise - ½ Cup
- Parmesan Cheese - 1 tbsp.
- Chopped Onion - 1 tbsp.
- Chopped Celery - 1 tbsp.
- Lemon Juice - ¼ Cup
- Oil - 1 tsp
- Dumplings Wrappers - 12

Preparation
1. Mix all Ingredients evenly.
2. Take dumplings wrappers and fill 1 tbsp. of mixture.
3. Carefully seal the edges.
4. Brush the oil and steam them for 15 minutes.
5. Serve with mint sauce.

Nutritional Facts
Calories: 1376 | Carbohydrates: 151g | Protein: 63g | Fat: 19g | Fiber: 6.1g |Cholesterol: 23.1mg | Sugar: 6g | Sodium: 3309mg

3.23 Cheesy Broccoli Rice Dumplings

Preparation Time: 25 minutes | Cooking Time: 10 minutes | Servings: 12

Ingredients
- Chopped Steamed Broccoli - ½ Cup
- Cooked Rice - 1 Cup
- Cheddar Cheese (Shred) - ¼ Cup
- Garlic Powder - 1 tsp
- Salt - ½ tsp
- Milk - 2 tbsp.
- Oil - 1 tbsp.
- Dumpling Wrappers - 12

Preparation
1. Combine all the Ingredients and mix them using hands.
2. Take dumpling wrappers and fill them with 1 tbsp. of mixture.
3. Stir fry in a nonstick skillet for 3-5 minutes.
4. Serve them with lemon dip.

Nutritional Facts
Calories: 1180 | Carbohydrates: 104g | Protein: 47g | Fat: 23.3g | Fiber: 15.3g |Cholesterol: 33mg | Sugar: 14g | Sodium: 2793mg

3.24 Wimey Timey Wontons

Preparation Time: 25 minutes | Cooking Time: 15 minutes | Servings: 12

Ingredients
- Mustard - 1 tbsp.
- Cornstarch - ½ tbsp.
- Milk - ½ Cup
- Mayonnaise - 1 tbsp.
- Lemon Juice - 1 tbsp.
- Dil - 1 tsp
- Black Pepper - ½ tsp
- Cayenne Pepper - 1 tsp
- Onion Powder - 1 tsp
- Bread Crumbs - ½ Cup
- Egg Yolk - 1
- Crumbled Tofu - 1 Cup
- Salt - ½ tsp
- Oil - 1 tsp
- Wonton Wrappers - 12

Preparation
1. Mix tofu and bread crumbs and mix well.
2. In a pan, heat milk and add cornstarch, mayo, mustard, spices, lemon juice, and egg. Whisk to make a delicate sauce and remove from heat.
3. Fill tofu mix in wonton wraps and seal them.
4. Steam wontons for 10-15 minutes.
5. Serve with mustard sauce.

Nutritional Facts
Calories: 1777 | Carbohydrates: 95.5g | Protein: 37g | Fat: 25g | Fiber: 3.3g | Cholesterol: 19mg | Sugar: 7.4 | Sodium: 3159mg

3.25 Cheese Potato Dumplings

Preparation Time: 25 minutes | Cooking Time: 10 minutes | Servings: 12

Ingredients
- potato(chopped) - 1 cup
- Cheese(shredded) - ½ cup
- Butter - 1tbsp
- onion(chopped) - ¼ cup
- Milk - ¼ cup
- Pepper - Pinch
- Salt - Pinch
- Wonton dumplings - 12
- Oil - For frying

Preparation
1. Mix all Ingredients in a large bowl.
2. Fill the dumplings.
3. Fry in preheated oil, until golden brown.
4. Serve hot.

Nutritional Facts
Calories: 1706 | Carbohydrates: 96g | Protein: 29g | Fat: 13g | Fiber: 7g | Cholesterol: 13mg | Sugar: 12.3g | Sodium: 2793mg

3.26 Spicy Beef & Veggie Dumplings

Preparation Time: 25 minutes | Cooking Time: 15 minutes | Servings: 12

Ingredients
- beef steak (chopped) - ½ cup
- carrots(chopped) - ½ cup
- green bell peppers(chopped) - ¼ cup
- cabbage(chopped) - ½ cup
- cilantro(chopped) - ¼ cup
- jalapeno pepper - 1tbsp
- Salt - 1tsp
- Scallions - ¼ cup
- soy sauce - 1tbsp
- Vinegar - 2tbsp
- lemon juice of 1 lemon
- dumpling wrappers - 10

Preparation
1. Mix all Ingredients in a large bowl.
2. Prepare the dumplings using the mixture, steam the dumplings until well done.
3. Serve hot with chili sauce.

Nutritional Facts
Calories: 1357 | Carbohydrates: 133g | Protein: 49g | Fat: 21g | Fiber: 13g | Cholesterol: 5.1mg | Sugar: 9.1g | Sodium: 1535mg

3.27 Cheese & Eggplant Dumplings

Preparation Time: 35 minutes | Cooking Time: 10 minutes | Servings: 12

Ingredients
- Eggplant (chopped) - 1 cup
- marinara sauce - 2tbsp
- Italian seasoning - 1tbsp
- onion powder - 1tbsp
- garlic powder - 1tsp
- Salt - Pinch
- parmesan cheese(shredded) - ¼ cup
- mozzarella cheese(shredded) - ¼ cup

- dumpling wrappers - 12
- marinara sauce - for dip

Preparation
1. Add all Ingredients to a food processor and give it a few rounds.
2. Fill in the mixture and form dumplings, fold the wrapper to half and form pleats.
3. Steam the dumplings in bamboo steamer.
4. Serve hot with marinara sauce.

Nutritional Facts
Calories: 1579 | Carbohydrates: 109g | Protein: 25.1g | Fat: 13.3g | Fiber: 17.1g | Cholesterol: 11.5mg | Sugar: 5.9g | Sodium: 3019mg

3.28 Parmesan Zucchini Dumplings

Preparation Time: 25 minutes | Cooking Time: 10 minutes | Servings: 15

Ingredients
- fresh parsley(chopped) - 1 tbsp.
- green onions(chopped) - 2
- garlic cloves(crushed) - 2
- Salt - 1 tbsp
- cherry tomatoes - ½ cup
- zucchini(chopped) - ½ cup
- fresh corn kernels - ½ cup
- eggplant(chopped) - ½ cup
- parmesan cheese - ¼ cup
- Oil - for frying
- dumpling wrappers - 15

Preparation
1. Add all Ingredients to a wok sauté.
2. Add them to a food processor, blend until flakey.
3. Prepare all the dumplings using the filling mixture.
4. Fry in preheat oil until golden brown.
5. Serve hot with Thai sweet chili sauce.

Nutritional Facts
Calories: 1972 | Carbohydrates: 198g | Protein: 41g | Fat: 55g | Fiber: 15.1g | Cholesterol: 3.1mg | Sugar: 19g | Sodium: 3745mg

3.29 Chicken & Vegetable Dumplings

Preparation Time: 25 minutes | Cooking Time: 20 minutes | Servings: 15

Ingredients
- chicken(boneless) - 1 cup
- carrots(chopped) - ½ cup
- cherry tomatoes(chopped) - ¼ cup
- potatoes (boiled & chopped) - ½ cup
- Sesame seeds - 1tsp
- soy sauce - 1tsp
- Pepper - 1tsp
- sea salt - pinch
- chicken broth - ¼ cup
- Oil - 2tbsp
- dumpling wrappers - 15

Preparation
1. Add chicken to a wok with oil and cook well.
2. Add all veggies and spices except broth, sauté and add broth let it dry on low flame.
3. Prepare all the dumplings with the mixture.
4. Steam the dumplings in a bamboo steamer until well done.
5. Serve hot.

Nutritional Facts
Calories: 947 | Carbohydrates: 107g | Protein: 51g | Fat: 21g | Fiber: 7.5g | Cholesterol: 11mg | Sugar: 7.5g | Sodium: 2971mg

3.30 Shiitake Mushroom and Thai Sauce Dumplings

Preparation Time: 35 minutes | Cooking Time: 10 minutes | Servings: 15

Ingredients
- Shiitake mushrooms(chopped) - 1 cup
- white peeper - 1tsp
- Chinese Chives(chopped) - 2
- garlic cloves(chopped) - 2
- soy sauce – 1 tbsp.
- white vinegar - 1tsp
- sesame oil - 1tsp
- tomatoes(chopped) - ½ cup
- red bell pepper(chopped) - ¼ cup
- green bell pepper(chopped) - ¼ cup
- eggplant(chopped) - ½ cup
- green chilies(chopped) - 2tbsp
- Thai sweet chili sauce - for dip
- Oil - for frying
- dumpling wrappers - 15

Preparation
1. Mix all Ingredients in a bowl and fill in the dumplings.
2. Deep fry the dumplings in pre-heated oil, until golden brown.
3. Serve with Thai sweet chili sauce.

Nutritional Facts
Calories: 1499 | Carbohydrates: 164g | Protein: 64g | Fat: 31g | Fiber: 13.1g | Cholesterol: 1.5mg | Sugar: 9.5 | Sodium: 3056mg

4 VEGAN DUMPLINGS

4.1 Cabbage Tofu Dumplings

Preparation Time: 25 minutes | Cooking Time: 10 minutes | Servings: 20

Ingredients

- Wonton wrappers - 20
- Cabbage - 150 g
- Firm tofu - 200 g
- Minced garlic - 10 g
- Oil - 1 tbsp.
- Soya sauce - 2 tbsp.
- Salt - ¼ tsp
- Star anise - 1
- Bay leave - 1
- Olive Oil - 2 tsp

Preparation

1. Take cabbage and dice it. Add 1/4 tsp salt and mix it. Squeeze cabbage to drain water
2. Take tofu and crush it.
3. In a pan add oil add minced garlic.
4. Sauté garlic and add tofu.
5. Add soya sauce in it and mix it. Add 1 bay leave and star anise.
6. Remove bay leave and star anise
7. When water dries from tofu it is ready
8. Drain excess water from cabbage again
9. Mix cabbage and tofu together.
10. Add this filling in wonton wrappers and boil for 10 minutes.
11. Serve them with your choice of Dip.

Nutritional Facts

Calories: 490 | Carbohydrates: 45g | Protein: 25g | Fat: 24g | Fiber: 8.5g | Cholesterol: 3.7mg | Sugar: 1.1g | Sodium: 3312mg

4.2 Dumplings with Chick Peas

Preparation Time: 25 minutes | Cooking Time: 5 minutes | Servings: 20

Ingredients

- Onion - 1
- Garlic - 4 oz.
- Carrot - 2 oz.
- Shitake Mushrooms – ½ cup
- Ginger - 1 oz.
- Soya Sauce - 1 oz.
- Salt and Pepper - ½ tsp
- Chickpeas - ½ tsp

- Sesame Oil - 2 Tsp
- Olive Oil - 2 Tsp

Preparation
4. Finely chop onion, carrots, mushrooms and boiled chickpeas.
5. Sauté them for 3 minutes.
6. Add salt and black pepper and soya sauce.
7. Put the mixture in dumplings wrappers.
8. Pour oil in pan and fry dumplings.
9. Serve them hot.

Nutritional Facts
Calories: 537 | Carbohydrates: 90g | Protein: 17g | Fat: 16.5g | Fiber: 3g |Cholesterol: 2.5mg | Sugar: 3g |Sodium: 2409mg

4.3 Crispy Bok Choy Dumpling

Preparation Time: 25 minutes | Cooking Time: 15 minutes | Servings: 20

Ingredients
- Bok Choy Roughly Chopped - 30 g
- Mushrooms Chopped- 5g
- Red Chili Chopped- 5g
- Sugar - 1tsp
- Garlic - 1
- Sesame Oil - 5ml
- Salt - ½ tsp

Preparation
1. Prepare the filling by blanching the chopped vegetables and mix well with rest of the Ingredients.
2. Cover the mixture and keep in the fridge.
3. Prepare the skin by using the potato starch and water to form a dough.
4. Cut and divide the dough in equal parts
5. Use a roller to make a wrapper.
6. Use the filling and fold it into dumplings.
7. Stir fry until golden brown. Serve hot.

Nutritional Facts
Calories: 401 | Carbohydrates: 39g | Protein: 11g | Fat: 13g | Fiber: 3.3g |Cholesterol: 1.5mg | Sugar: 4.1g |Sodium: 1991mg

4.4 Mixed Vegetable Filled Dumplings

Preparation Time: 15 minutes | Cooking Time: 50 minutes | Servings: 25

Preparation
- Glass noodles - 25g
- Mushrooms - 220g
- Ginger - 2 oz.
- Garlic cloves - 3
- Salt – ¼ tsp
- Soy sauce - 1 tbsp.
- Salt - ½ tsp
- Carrot - 200g
- Sweet corns - 75g
- Sesame oil - 1 tsp

Preparation
1. Take glass noodles and soak it in boiling water for 10 minutes.
2. Cut stems of mushrooms and cut into thick slices. Mince ginger and garlic into puree.
3. Roast carrots in 200°C oven for 20 minutes.
4. Stir fry mushrooms with ginger, garlic and small amount of oil. Add salt, soy sauce and cook for 5 minutes.
5. Add cooked mushrooms, carrots and glass noodles in blender and blend in small pieces. Add corns to the mixture.
6. Put this mixture in dumpling wrappers. Steam them for 10-15 minutes.
7. Serve with choice of dip.

Nutritional Facts
Calories: 523 | Carbohydrates: 79g | Protein: 15g | Fat: 12.5g | Fiber: 2.9g |Cholesterol: 2mg | Sugar: 1.5g |Sodium: 2107mg

4.5 Olive Green Bean Filled Dumplings

Preparation Time: 25 minutes | Cooking Time: 10 minutes | Servings: 30

Ingredients
- Green beans - 220g
- Chinese olive vegetables - 30g
- Oil - 2 oz.
- Water – ½ cup

Preparation
1. Cut off the string ends and then cut into small pieces.
2. Stir fry green beans with Chinese oil vegetable sand a small amount of oil and add enough water to cover green beans and then cook with a lid on for 10 minutes until beans are soft.
3. Add cooked beans into food processor and blend into paste.
4. Fill this in dumplings and stir fry them for 5 minutes.
5. Serve them with your favorite dip.

Nutritional Facts

Calories: 255 | Carbohydrates: 29g | Protein: 9g | Fat: 7g | Fiber: 2.9g | Cholesterol: 0.1mg | Sugar: 1.1g | Sodium: 1709mg

4.6 Paper Dumplings

Preparation Time: 25 minutes | Cooking Time: 15 minutes | Servings: 30

Ingredients

- Mushrooms - 4 oz.
- Soya sauce - 2 oz.
- Honey - ½ tsp
- Cabbage - 1 oz.
- Carrots - 1 oz.
- Salt - ½ tsp
- Pepper - ½ tsp
- Rice paper sheets - 10
- Olive Oil - 2 tsp

Preparation

1. Finely chop carrots, mushrooms and cabbage.
2. Add little bit of oil and fry it for 3 minutes.
3. Add salt, pepper, soya sauce and chili sauce.
4. Dip rice paper in water.
5. Add mixture in center of rice paper and fold from sides. Again wrap it with one more rice sheet.
6. Add oil in pan and then pan fry dumplings from both sides. They are ready to serve.

Nutritional Facts

Calories: 577 | Carbohydrates: 71g | Protein: 13g | Fat: 17g | Fiber: 3.7g | Cholesterol: 2.5mg | Sugar: 3.1g | Sodium: 3123mg

4.7 Oatmeal Maple Gyoza

Preparation Time: 35 minutes | Cooking Time: 15 minutes | Servings: 30

Ingredients

- Tofu crumbled - 14 oz.
- Cabbage finely chopped - 2 leaves
- Ginger minced - 1
- Carrot small - 1
- Mushrooms - 100 g
- Green onion - 1
- Oatmeal - 2 tsp
- Pepper - ¼ tsp
- Sesame Oil - 1tsp
- Salt - ¼ tsp
- Soy sauce - 1 tbsp.
- Vinegar - 1 tbsp.

- Maple syrup - 1 tbsp.
- Ginger (sliced) - 2 tbsp.

Preparation
1. Take tofu and crush it finely. Add finely chopped carrots, cabbage, ginger and green onion.
2. Add soya sauce, pepper, salt and sesame oil.
3. Mix all Ingredients evenly.
4. Add mixture in the center of dumpling wrapper and seal ends with water.
5. In a pan add 1 tbsp. oil and 1/3 cup of water in pan and add 13 gyozas in pan.
6. When water is evaporated then pan fry for 1 min more.
7. For dipping sauce add soya sauce, vinegar maple syrup and ginger slices.

Nutritional Facts

Calories: 701 | Carbohydrates: 972g | Protein: 21g | Fat: 19g | Fiber: 5.5g | Cholesterol: 3mg | Sugar: 5.7g | Sodium: 3783mg

4.8 Chili Oil Wontons

Preparation Time: 45 minutes | Cooking Time: 15 minutes | Servings: 30

Ingredients
- Spinach - 50 gm
- Tofu - 50g
- Mushrooms - 4 pieces dried
- Green onion - 1
- Ginger - 10g
- Salt - ½ tsp
- Sugar - 1 tbsp.
- Sesame Oil - 1 tbsp.
- Vegetable broth - 500 ml
- Soya sauce - 1 tbsp.
- Sesame oil - 1 tsp
- Chili oil - 2 tbsp.
- Minced garlic - 1 tsp
- Sichuan pepper powder - 1 tsp

Preparation
1. Soak mushrooms in warm water for at least 1 hour then squeeze them and chop finely.
2. Cut spring onion into rings and chop the ginger. Crush tofu with fork.
3. Heat oil then fry mushrooms, onion and ginger in it. Add spinach and sesame oil, mix them well.
4. Bring some soup to boil. Carefully place wontons in boiling soup and cook for 5-7 minutes till wontons float to the surface.
5. Mix soya sauce, Sichuan sauce, garlic chili oil and sesame oil in a bowl.

Nutritional Facts

Calories: 753 | Carbohydrates: 113g | Protein: 27g | Fat: 23g | Fiber: 5.7g | Cholesterol: 3.3mg | Sugar: 4.1g | Sodium: 3551mg

4.9 Spring Vegetable Pot stickers

Preparation Time: 25 minutes | Cooking Time: 10 minutes | Servings: 25

Ingredients
- Onion - 1oz
- Ginger - 1 tbsp.
- Peas - 1 cup
- Garlic - 1 tbsp.
- Asparagus - 1 cup
- Salt and pepper - ½ tsp
- Spinach chopped - 3 cups
- Sesame Oil - 2 tsp
- Soya sauce - 2 tbsp.

Preparation
1. Heat oil in a large pan and add onion, ginger and garlic. Cook until onion is translucent.
2. Add asparagus, carrots, cabbage and peas and stir. Cook for 3 minutes.
3. Cook spinach until it is tender.
4. Remove the filling from the heat and transfer to a large mixing bowl, then stir until thoroughly incorporated.
5. Fill the dumpling wrappers with the filling mixture.
6. In a large skillet, heat 1 tablespoon of oil over low heat and add dumplings. Cook for four minutes, or until a crust forms. Add a quarter cup of water to the pan, then cover with a lid.
7. For 6 to 8 minutes, steam. Warm them up.

Nutritional Facts
Calories: 491 | Carbohydrates: 47g | Protein: 27g | Fat: 19g | Fiber: 5.1g | Cholesterol: 3mg | Sugar: 3g | Sodium: 3103mg

4.10 Sweet Potato Chive Wontons

Preparation Time: 25 minutes | Cooking Time: 15 minutes | Servings: 12

Ingredients
- Chinese garlic Chive - 80g
- Oil - 1 tbsp.
- Salt - 1 tsp
- Cook sweet potato - 160g
- Sesame paste - 1 tbsp.
- Wonton wrappers - 12

Preparation
1. Chop the Chinese garlic chive into small pieces and stir fry with little oil and salt until it softens.
2. Use a fork to soften the mash potato into a paste, and the sesame sauces and mix then add the cooked garlic chive. Taste the salt if needed.
3. Fill the mixture in wonton wrappers.
4. Steam wontons for 10-15 minutes and serve them.

Nutritional Facts: Calories: 377 | Carbohydrates: 41g | Protein: 12g | Fat: 13g | Fiber: 5g | Cholesterol: 2.5mg | Sugar: 1.7 | Sodium: 2331mg

4.11 Truffle Mushrooms

Preparation Time: 35 minutes | Cooking Time: 10 minutes | Servings: 6

Ingredients
- Beech mushrooms - 1
- King oyster mushrooms - 4 oz.
- Oil - 2 oz.
- Salt – ½ cup
- Black pepper - 1 oz.
- Soya sauce - 1 oz.
- Chopped spring onions - ½ tsp
- Truffle oil - 1 tsp
- Maple syrup - 1 tsp
- Dumpling Wraps - 6

Preparation
1. Cut off the bottom of the beech mushrooms and king oyster mushroom into dices.
2. Fry mushrooms with small amount of oil.
3. Add black pepper soya sauce, salt and truffle oil.
4. To make filling and add cooked mushrooms into food processor and mix well with chopped green onions.
5. Fill mixture in the dumpling wrappers and stir fry them for 3-5 minutes.
6. Dish out with lemon juice on top.

Nutritional Facts Calories: 567 | Carbohydrates: 41g | Protein: 14g | Fat: 11g | Fiber: 5.1g |Cholesterol: 1.7mg | Sugar: 3.7g |Sodium: 1907mg

4.12 Veg Dim Sum

Preparation Time: 25 minutes | Cooking Time: 15 minutes | Servings: 15

Ingredients
- Cabbage - 1 oz.
- Carrot - 1 oz.
- Salt - ½ tsp
- Pepper - ½ tsp
- Soya Sauce - 2 tsp
- Red Chilies - 2 tsp
- Sesame Oil - ½ tsp
- Spring Greens - 1 tbsp.

Preparation
1. In a bowl add cabbage, carrots, green onions salt and crushed black pepper.
2. Add the filling in the dumpling wrappers and apply little water at the ends to seal.
3. Take a pan and fill it with water and on top of it take a sieve and cover it.
4. Take Cabbage leaf over it and keep dim sum on it and cover the lid.
5. Let steam for 15 minutes.
6. In a small bowl add soya sauce, red chilies, sesame oil and green onions. Pour this sauce of steamed dumplings.

Nutritional Facts
Calories: 375 | Carbohydrates: 30g | Protein: 10g | Fat: 8g | Fiber: 1.1g | Cholesterol: 0.9mg | Sugar: 1.5g | Sodium: 1799mg

4.13 Maple Syrup and Tofu Dumplings

Preparation Time: 25 minutes | Cooking Time: 20 minutes | Servings: 12

Ingredients
- Cabbage (finely chopped) - 1cup
- Tofu – 6 oz.
- bay leaves - 2
- garlic cloves(crushed) - 2
- scallions(chopped) - 1tbsp
- ginger(grated) - 1tsp
- jalapeno(chopped) - 2
- Salt - 1tsp
- soy sauce - 2tsp
- maple syrup - 2tbsp
- Vinegar - 2tsp
- Butter - 2tbsp
- dumpling wrappers - 12

Preparation
1. Mince tofu using fingers; add butter in a wok with garlic, ginger, scallions and sauté.
2. Add tofu, cook adding spices and sauces, until water is dried.

3. Remove from flame and let it cool.
4. Mix all Ingredients in bowl, fill the dumpling wrappers and fold the dumplings, steam in a bamboo steamer.
5. Serve hot with sweet chili sauce.

Nutritional Facts
Calories: 591 | Carbohydrates: 57g | Protein: 37g | Fat: 29g | Fiber: 7g | Cholesterol: 5mg | Sugar: 4.1g | Sodium: 3191mg

4.14 Glass Noodle and Cherry Tomato Dumpling

Preparation Time: 35 minutes | Cooking Time: 15 minutes | Servings: 15

Ingredients
- Salt - 1tsp
- black pepper - 1tbsp
- cherry tomatoes(chopped) - ½ cup
- corn kernels - 2tbsp
- shiitake mushrooms(chopped) - 1cup
- carrots(chopped) - ½ cup
- glass noodles(softened) - 1cup
- Butter - 1tbsp
- Oil - for frying
- dumpling wrappers - 15

Preparation
1. Add butter to a pan and fry mushrooms until softened, let it cool.
2. Add all Ingredients to a food processor and give it 2-3 rounds.
3. Fill in the wrappers and deep fry until golden brown.
4. Serve hot.

Nutritional Facts
Calories: 768 | Carbohydrates: 71g | Protein: 51g | Fat: 21g | Fiber: 9g | Cholesterol: 3.9mg | Sugar: 5.9g | Sodium: 3763mg

5 BEEF DUMPLINGS

5.1 Beef Steamed Dumplings

Preparation Time: 45 minutes | Cooking Time: 15 minutes | Servings: 30

Ingredients
- fresh ginger - 2-inch
- Szechuan peppercorns - 1 tsp
- ground beef - ½ lb.
- chicken stock - ¼ cup
- soy sauce - 1 tbsp.
- kosher salt - ½ tsp
- boiling water - 1 cup
- Flour - 2½ cup
- frozen peas - ½ cup
- Carrot - 1 med
- green onions - 4
- vegetable oil - 2 tbsp.

Preparation
1. Grind the peppercorns in a grinder
2. Mix peppercorns with ginger, ground beef, soy sauce, rice water, and salt.
3. Chop the green onions and carrots finely. Mix the ground beef and processed veggies.
4. Fill in the dumpling wrappers and seal with any method you like.
5. Heat vegetable oil over medium heat. Add 3 tablespoons of water and cover it with a lid. Dumplings should be cooked through after 3 minutes of steaming. For each batch of dumplings, repeat the process.
6. Your choice of dipping sauce is optional.

Nutritional Facts
Calories: 1317| Carbohydrates: 113g | Protein: 78.4g | Fat: 99.5g | Fiber: 19.1g |Cholesterol: 25.2mg | Sugar: 11.3g |Sodium: 2133mg

5.2 Beef Fried Dumplings

Preparation Time: 25 minutes | Cooking Time: 20 minutes | Servings: 30

Ingredients
- Ground beef - 1 lb.
- Onion - ½ cup
- Scallion - ½ cup
- Soy sauce - 2 tbsp.
- Cloves garlic - 2
- Grated ginger - 2 tsp
- White pepper – 1 tbsp.
- Egg wash - 2½ cup

Preparation

1. Combine ground beef, scallions, soy sauce, onions, garlic, grated ginger, sesame oil and white pepper.
2. Put the ground beef mix in the center of the wrapper, brush the edges with egg wash, fold over, and seal.
3. The dumplings should be fried until golden brown and crispy.
4. Serve with Sriracha sauce and chopped scallions.
5. Have fun!

Nutritional Facts

Calories: 1740 | Carbohydrates: 145g | Protein:86 g | Fat: 101g | Fiber: 15g |Cholesterol: 33.5mg | Sugar: 3g |Sodium: 2900mg

5.3 Northern Chinese Beef

- Preparation Time: 35 minutes | Cooking Time: 15 minutes | Servings: 30

Ingredients

- Beef mince - 500g
- Carrot - 2
- Button mushrooms - 10
- Eggs - 3
- Spring onions - 3
- Ginger - 1
- Soy sauce - 2 tbsp.
- Oyster sauce - 1 tsp
- Sesame oil - 1 tsp
- Vegetable oil – 1/3 cup
- Spring onions - 1 bunch
- Rice vinegar - 2tsp

Preparation

1. Cook mushrooms, carrot, and eggs over medium heat for 1-2 minutes.
2. Combine egg mix and all the remaining Ingredients.
3. Fill dumplings and fry for two minutes, or until the bottoms are golden brown and crunchy.
4. Add enough water to cover the dumplings halfway, then cover with a lid.
5. Cook until all of the liquid has evaporated and the dumplings are tender.
6. Serve dumplings with sweet and sour sauce.

Nutritional Facts

Calories: 2140 | Carbohydrates: 162g | Protein: 122g | Fat: 154g | Fiber: 5g |Cholesterol: 14mg | Sugar: 2g |Sodium: 1707mg

5.4 Pan-Fried Chinese Beef Dumplings

Preparation Time: 35 minutes | Cooking Time: 15 minutes | Servings: 30

Ingredients
- Cumin seeds - 200g
- Sichuan peppercorns - 200g
- Beef mince - 1 lb.
- Soy sauce – 1 tsp
- Garlic clove - 1
- Chopped coriander - 3 tbsp.
- Grated ginger - 1 tbsp.
- Corn flour - 1 tsp
- Water - 2 tbsp.

Preparation
1. Fry cumin seeds and Sichuan peppercorns ad grind them. Add and mix the remaining fillings.
2. Put two heaping teaspoons of filling in the center of a wrapper. Seal the edges.
3. After boiling the dumplings, immediately pour in the room temperature water.
4. For about 4 minutes, cook until done.
5. Transfer the dumplings to serving bowls using a slotted spoon. Add soy sauce and chili oil.
6. Garnish coriander and spring onion, and serve.

Nutritional Facts
Calories: 1540 | Carbohydrates: 105g | Protein: 97g | Fat: 111g | Fiber: 6g | Cholesterol: 120mg | Sugar: 9g | Sodium: 2501mg

5.5 Beef Chili Dumplings

Preparation Time: 25 minutes | Cooking Time: 20 minutes | Servings: 30

Ingredients
- Vegetable oil - 1 tbsp.
- Beef mince - 500g
- Garlic cloves - 2
- Ginger - 1 tbsp.
- Red chili finely chopped - 2 small
- Soy sauce - 1 tbsp.
- Oyster sauce - 1 tbsp.
- Dumpling wrappers - 275g / 1packet
- Green onion - 5
- Butter - 30g
- Sesame oil - 1 tbsp.

Preparation
1. Heat oil over medium-high heat.
2. Add garlic, ginger and chili. Stir-fry for 5 minutes
3. Make dumplings with the wrapper.

4. Place dumplings in water and then cook for half hour.
5. Shred onions. heat butter and sesame oil and add chili in it. cook and stir for a minute.
6. Put the dumplings in place with remaining mince mixture and serve.

Nutritional Facts

Calories: 1247 | Carbohydrates: 75g | Protein: 83g | Fat: 66g | Fiber: 6.3g | Cholesterol: 37mg | Sugar: 31 | Sodium: 2221mg

5.6 Steamed Beef Dumplings

Preparation Time: 25 minutes | Cooking Time: 25 minutes | Servings: 30

Ingredients

- ground beef - 20 oz.
- chicken stock - ½ cup
- soy sauce - 3 tbsp.
- Salt - 1 tsp
- white pepper - ½ tsp
- grated ginger - 1 tbsp.
- Green, yellow onion - 2 stalks
- celery – 8-10 stalks
- sesame oil - 1 tbsp.
- olive oil - 1 tbsp.

Preparation

1. Mix all the Ingredients and blanch the celery in boiling water and then cut it into slices.
2. Combine celery, olive oil, sesame oil and other Ingredients into the beef filling.
3. Place filling inside it and press it so that the filling is completely sealed inside.
4. Start boiling water in a pan.
5. Wet a coffee filter and line your steamer basket.
6. Wet the coffee filters and place the dumplings on them. For 12-15 minutes, steam.
7. Let the dumplings cool and then enjoy.

Nutritional Facts

Calories: 1240 | Carbohydrates: 98g | Protein: 62g | Fat: 25g | Fiber: 4.5g | Cholesterol: 79mg | Sugar: 35 | Sodium: 3901mg

5.7 Beef Carrot Dumplings

Preparation Time: 25 minutes | Cooking Time: 15 minutes | Servings: 12

Ingredients

- ground beef - 1 lb.
- Carrots - 2 small
- Red onion - 1 small
- Scallion - 2
- White pepper - ½ tsp
- Salt - ½ tsp
- Ginger - 1 inch

- soy sauce - ½ tsp
- Shaoxing wine - 1 tsp

Preparation
1. Mix beef and all spices together.
2. Add onion, carrot, scallion, sesame oil and ginger in it.
3. Make the dumplings and fill in the center and press the corners.
4. Repeat the process.
5. Put the dumplings in steamer with boiling water for few minutes.
6. Serve them with black vinegar.

Nutritional Facts
Calories: 1840 | Carbohydrates: 109g | Protein: 87g | Fat: 99g | Fiber: 5.5g | Cholesterol: 37mg | Sugar: 7.3 | Sodium: 3160mg

5.8 Special Chinese Dumplings

Preparation Time: 25 minutes | Cooking Time: 20 minutes | Servings: 12

Ingredients
- ground beef - 1 lb.
- Chinese cabbage - 2 cup
- Carrot - 1 med.
- Onion - 1 med.
- Egg - 1 large
- soy sauce - 1 tbsp.
- vegetable oil - 1 tbsp.
- sugar - 1 tsp
- salt - 1 tsp

Preparation
1. Mix together cabbage, beef, carrot and onion in a bowl and stir with egg, soy sauce, oil, sugar and salt.
2. Make the dumplings and put the filling in the wrapper.
3. Put few drops of water to soften.
4. Repeat the process.
5. Put the water to boil and add dumplings to cook for 5 minutes approximately. Serve them.

Nutritional Facts
Calories: 2040 | Carbohydrates: 109g | Protein: 91g | Fat: 103g | Fiber: 5.3g | Cholesterol: 55mg | Sugar: 7.3 | Sodium: 3177mg

5.9 Quick Beef Dumplings

- Preparation Time: 35 minutes | Cooking Time: 15 minutes | Servings: 12

Ingredients
- ground chuck - 1lb.
- Scallions - 4
- Egg - 1
- Low sodium soy sauce - 3 tbsp.

Preparation
1. Place beef, scallions, water and soy sauce in a bowl and mix.
2. Put the filling in dumpling wrapper with beaten egg to seal ends.
3. Place dumplings in the heated oil and fry for 3 minutes.
4. Add the required amount of water and cover pan.
5. Cook until water evaporates.
6. Serve when cooked.

Nutritional Facts
Calories: 1357 | Carbohydrates: 33g | Protein: 77g | Fat: 79g | Fiber: 5.5g | Cholesterol: 131mg | Sugar: 3.5g | Sodium: 1901mg

5.10 Russian Meat Dumpling

- Preparation Time: 45 minutes | Cooking Time: 20 minutes | Servings: 12

Ingredients
- Eggs - 2 large
- Water – 2/3 cup
- vegetable oil - 1 tbsp.
- kosher salt – ½ tsp
- purpose flour – 3¼ cup
- Onion - 1 large
- ground lean pork - 8 oz.
- ground beef chuck - 8 oz.

Preparation
1. Mix all the Ingredients and mix egg, water, oil, salt and flour.
2. Add flour and make the dough.
3. Knead the dough and wrap it
4. Mix onion, beef or lean pork, salt, pepper together.
5. Fill the mixture in dumplings and fry it in the oil until cooked.
6. Ready to serve now.

Nutritional Facts
Calories: 2041 | Carbohydrates: 119g | Protein: 97g | Fat: 109g | Fiber: 5.5g | Cholesterol: 51.1mg | Sugar: 7.3g | Sodium: 3167mg

5.11 Sunflower Beef Dumplings

Preparation Time: 40 minutes | Cooking Time: 15 minutes | Servings: 12

Ingredients
- sunflower oil - 2 tbsp.
- Scotch Beef mince - ½ cup
- garlic cloves - 2
- Ginger - 1 tsp
- red chilies - 2 small
- oyster sauce - 2 tbsp.
- dumpling wrappers - 12
- spring onions - 3

Preparation
1. Heat sunflower oil and mix the mince, garlic, ginger and chili and cook. Mix oyster sauce and cool it.
2. Mix the filling in the kneaded dough and make dumplings.
3. Brush edges with water and fold the dumplings.
4. Repeat the process and put in slightly boiled water for 30 seconds.
5. Heat the oil and cook spring onions and chili.
6. Mix the sauce and sesame seeds with lemon juice in bowl.
7. Put dumplings in plate and spread onion and serve with sauce.

Nutritional Facts
Calories: 1461 | Carbohydrates: 101g | Protein: 78g | Fat: 89g | Fiber: 7.2g | Cholesterol: 33mg | Sugar: 9g | Sodium: 2371mg

5.12 Beef Steak Dumplings

Preparation Time: 35 minutes | Cooking Time: 1 hour 15 minutes | Servings: 12

Ingredients
- Beef steak - ½ cup
- Pepper – ¼ tsp
- canola oil - 2 tsp
- chicken soup - 2/3 cup
- beef broth – ½ cup
- fresh mushroom - 4 large
- onion, green pepper and celery - ¼ cup

Preparation
1. Brown or fry steak in oil and mix soup, broth and vegetables over it. Cook for 1 hour.
2. Make dumplings by mixing and kneading the flour.
3. Sprinkle with parsley.
4. Stir in egg and milk until blended.
5. Cover and cook on high flame.

Nutritional Facts: Calories: 1269 | Carbohydrates: 81g | Protein: 69g | Fat: 87g | Fiber: 3.2g | Cholesterol: 13.3mg | Sugar: 5.3 | Sodium: 2191mg

5.13 Jalapeno Beef Dumplings

Preparation Time: 25 minutes | Cooking Time: 25 minutes | Servings: 12

Ingredients
- ground beef - 1cup
- garlic cloves(crushed) - 2
- Scallions - 1tbsp.
- ginger(grated) - 1tsp
- jalapeno(chopped) - 2
- sea salt - 1tsp
- soy sauce - 1tsp
- white vinegar - 1tsp
- Oil - 2tbsp
- dumpling wrappers - 12

Preparation
1. Sauté garlic, scallions and ginger in 2tbsp oil, and beef and cook for until color changes.
2. Add to it all Ingredients, remove from flame and let it cool.
3. Fill the wrappers and fold the dumplings, steam in a bamboo steamer.
4. Serve hot with Thai chili sauce.

Nutritional Facts
Calories: 1460 | Carbohydrates: 99g | Protein: 72g | Fat: 88g | Fiber: 7g |Cholesterol: 31mg | Sugar: 8g |Sodium: 2200mg

5.14 Beef & Corn Dumpling

- Preparation Time: 25 minutes | Cooking Time: 25 minutes | Servings: 12

Ingredients
- ground beef - 1cup
- corn kernels - ¼ cup
- garlic cloves(pressed) - 2
- ginger paste - 1tbsp
- onions(chopped) - ½ cup
- Chinese 5 spice powder - 1tsp
- Sichuan peppercorns(ground) - 1tsp
- Salt - Pinch
- dumpling wrappers - 12
- Oil - for frying
- Chinese chili sauce - for dip sauce

Preparation
1. Add chopped onions, garlic cloves and ginger paste in a wok, with oil.
2. Toast corn kernels, add ground beef and spices. Heat all until well cooked.
3. Remove from flame and let it cool.
4. Fill the mixture and form dumplings, fry in preheated oil, until golden brown.

5. Serve with Chinese chili sauce.

Nutritional Facts: Calories: 2140 | Carbohydrates: 129g | Protein: 107g | Fat: 119g | Fiber: 6.5g | Cholesterol: 55mg | Sugar: 8.3g | Sodium: 3560mg

5.15 Mushroom Beef Dumplings

- Preparation Time: 25 minutes | Cooking Time: 25 minutes | Servings: 12

Ingredients
- mushrooms(chopped) - ½ cup
- beef(ground) - 1cup
- cilantro(chopped) - ¼ cup
- carrots(chopped) - ½ cup
- soy sauce - 1tbsp
- rice wine - 1tbsp
- Pepper - pinch
- Salt - 1tsp
- Peanuts (finely chopped) - 2tbsp
- Oil - 2tbsp
- dumpling wrappers - 12

Preparation
1. Add oil in a wok with spices and veggies, sauté, then add beef and cook for 2-5 min.
2. Let the mixture cool down.
3. Fill in the dumplings with the filling mixture.
4. Steam the dumplings in a steamer.
5. Serve hot with chili sauce.

Nutritional Facts
Calories: 1348 | Carbohydrates: 109g | Protein: 71g | Fat: 97g | Fiber: 6g | Cholesterol: 35.7mg | Sugar: 8.6g | Sodium: 3510mg

5.16 Pear Beef Dumplings with Honey

- Preparation Time: 25 minutes | Cooking Time: 15 minutes | Servings: 12

Ingredients
- beef(ground) - ½ cup
- Honey – 2 tbsp.
- Pear - 1 med sized
- Parsley - 1tsp
- Butter – 1 tbsp.
- Salt - Pinch
- wonton dumplings - 12
- oil - for frying

Preparation
1. Add all Ingredients to a food processor, blend well.
2. Fill the mixture in the dumplings.
3. Fry them in preheated oil.
4. Serve hot.

Nutritional Facts
Calories: 1169 | Carbohydrates: 80g | Protein: 68g | Fat: 85g | Fiber: 3.2g | Cholesterol: 13mg | Sugar: 6.3 | Sodium: 2390mg

5.17 Korean Beef Dumplings

- Preparation Time: 25 minutes | Cooking Time: 15 minutes | Servings: 10

Ingredients
- bean sprouts(chopped) - ¼ cup
- beef(ground) - 1cup
- cabbage(chopped) - ½ cup
- green onions(chopped) - 2
- tofu(chopped) - ¼ cup
- salt - pinch
- black pepper - 1tsp
- Oil - for frying
- dumpling wrapper - 10
- Chinese chili sauce - for dip sauce

Preparation
1. Add bean sprouts with onions in a pan and sauté add beef and all other Ingredients, cook well.
2. Prepare all the dumplings using the filling mixture, fry until light brown color appears.
3. Serve hot.

Nutritional Facts
Calories: 1893 | Carbohydrates: 88g | Protein: 42g | Fat: 60g | Fiber: 4.4g | Cholesterol: 35mg | Sugar: 4.9g | Sodium: 1760mg

5.18 Chicken & Beef Dumpling

Preparation Time: 25 minutes | Cooking Time: 30 minutes | Servings: 15

Ingredients
- chicken(boneless) - 1 cup
- beef(ground) - ½ cup
- soy sauce - 1tsp
- Pepper - 1tsp
- sea salt - pinch
- chicken broth - ¼ cup
- Shao sing wine - 1tbsp
- Thai sweet chili sauce - for dip sauce
- Oil - 2tbsp
- dumpling wrappers - 15

Preparation
1. Add beef to a wok with oil, cook well.
2. Add all other Ingredients except broth, sauté and add broth let it dry on low flame.
3. Prepare all the dumplings using the filling mixture, steam the dumplings until well done.
4. Serve hot with Thai sweet chili sauce.

Nutritional Facts
Calories: 1980 | Carbohydrates: 99g | Protein: 52g | Fat: 79g | Fiber: 4.2g | Cholesterol: 55mg | Sugar: 5.2g | Sodium: 2150mg

5.19 Yummy Beef Dumplings

Preparation Time: 35 minutes | Cooking Time: 15 minutes | Servings: 12

Ingredients
- beef steak (mild done/chopped) - ½ cup
- cilantro(chopped) - ¼ cup
- jalapeno pepper - 1tsp
- Salt - pinch
- Scallions - ¼ cup
- Vinegar - 1tbsp
- lemon juice - 1 lemon
- fish sauce or hoisin sauce - 2tbsp
- dumpling wrappers - 10

Preparation
1. Mix all Ingredients in a large bowl.
2. Prepare the dumplings using the filling, steam the dumplings until well done.
3. Serve hot, in a nice platter.

Nutritional Facts Calories: 985 | Carbohydrates: 49g | Protein: 28g | Fat: 51g | Fiber: 3.7g | Cholesterol: 32mg | Sugar: 3.9g | Sodium: 1598mg

5.20 Fajita Beef Dumplings

Preparation Time: 35 minutes | Cooking Time: 20 minutes | Servings: 12

Ingredients

- Onion - ¼ Cup
- Beef Chopped - 1 Cup
- Cheese - 1 Cup
- Bell Pepper - ¼ Cup
- Garlic Powder - ½ tsp
- Cayenne Pepper - ¼ tsp
- Salt - 1 tsp
- Oil - For Frying
- Chili Powder - 2 tsp
- Cumin - ½ tsp
- Dumpling Wraps - 12

Preparation

1. Cook beef for 10-15 minutes in a skillet with salt, garlic powder, and chili powder.
2. Take all Ingredients and mix them with beef.
3. Put oil in the pot and start filling the dumpling wrappers.
4. Deep fry dumplings for 5 minutes until they turn golden brown.
5. Serve with guacamole sauce.

Nutritional Facts

Calories: 1740 | Carbohydrates: 137g | Protein: 78g | Fat: 115g | Fiber: 5.7g | Cholesterol: 58mg | Sugar: 6.5g | Sodium: 2950mg

5.21 Beef Teriyaki Wontons

Preparation Time: 25 minutes | Cooking Time: 20 minutes | Servings: 12

Ingredients

- Cooked Beef - 1 Cup
- Soy Sauce - ½ Cup
- Sugar - ½ Cup
- Cornstarch - 1 tbsp.
- Water - 1 tbsp.
- Apple cider Vinegar - ¼ Cup
- Black Pepper - ¼ tsp
- Ginger Chopped - ½ tsp
- Chopped Garlic - ½ tsp
- Oil - 3 tbsp.
- Teriyaki Sauce - 2 tbsp.
- Wonton Wraps - 12

Preparation
1. Cook Soy sauce, Sugar, Water, and Vinegar. Bring them to a boil.
2. Add beef and teriyaki sauce and mix them finally.
3. Fill the mixture in the dumplings.
4. Fry for 4-5 minutes and serve with red chili sauce.

Nutritional Facts
Calories: 1650 | Carbohydrates: 86g | Protein: 23g | Fat: 65g | Fiber: 6.5g | Cholesterol: 59mg | Sugar: 5.5g | Sodium: 2707mg

5.22 Beef Sausage Dumplings

Preparation Time: 25 minutes | Cooking Time: 20 minutes | Servings: 12

Ingredients
- Onion - ¼ Cup
- Celery - ¼ Cup
- Carrot - ¼ Cup
- Chopped Beef Sausages - 1 Cup
- Parmesan Cheese - ¼ Cup
- Italian Seasonings - 1 tsp
- Garlic Cloves - 2
- Oil - 1 Cup
- Dumpling Wraps - 12

Preparation
1. Sauté sausages and then add vegetables and seasonings.
2. Remove from heat and add cheese.
3. Fill the mixture in the dumpling wrappers and seal them.
4. Deep fry dumplings until they are crispy.
5. Garnish until green chives.

Nutritional Facts
Calories: 660 | Carbohydrates: 39g | Protein: 13g | Fat: 25g | Fiber: 3.6g | Cholesterol: 35mg | Sugar: 3.7g | Sodium: 1150mg

5.23 Swedish Beef Dumplings with Gravy

Preparation Time: 35 minutes | Cooking Time: 20 minutes | Servings: 30

Ingredients
- Beef Booth - 1 Cup
- Sour Cream - ¼ Cup
- All Purpose Flour - 2 tbsp.
- Unsalted-Butter - 1 tbsp.
- Chopped Onions - ¼ Cup
- Egg - 1
- Milk - ¼ Cup
- Bread crumbs - ¼ Cup

- Parsley - 1 tsp
- Worcestershire Sauce - 1 tsp
- Salt - 1 tsp
- Black Pepper - ½ tsp
- Oil - 3 tbsp.
- Beef Cooked - ½ lb.
- Dumpling Wrapper - 12

Preparation
1. In a pan, Melt butter and add all-purpose flour and gently whisk to avoid lumps. Add sour cream and set aside.
2. Combine all the remaining Ingredients and fill in the dumpling wraps. Stir fry in oil for 3-5 minutes.
3. Serve with thickened gravy on top. Garnish with scallions.

Nutritional Facts
Calories: 1422 | Carbohydrates: 84g | Protein: 42g | Fat: 75g | Fiber: 8.5g | Cholesterol: 93mg | Sugar: 3.7g | Sodium: 2901mg

5.24 Beef Buffalo Wraps

Preparation Time: 35 minutes | Cooking Time: 15 minutes | Servings: 30

Ingredients
- Shredded Cooked Beef 1 Cup
- Chopped Celery - ¼ Cup
- Chopped Carrot - ¼ Cup
- Blue Cheese Shred - 2 tbsp.
- Buffalo Sauce - 2 tbsp.
- Oil - 1 Cup
- Dumpling Wraps - 12

Preparation
1. Mix all the above Ingredients and fill the mixture in the dumpling wrappers.
2. Seal them by using instructions.
3. Fry dumplings for 4-5 minutes and dish them out with buffalo sauce.

Nutritional Facts
Calories: 947 | Carbohydrates: 67g | Protein: 27g | Fat: 57g | Fiber: 4.5g | Cholesterol: 66mg | Sugar: 3.8g | Sodium: 1776mg

6 PORK DUMPLINGS

6.1 Green Thai Curry Dumplings

Preparation Time: 45 minutes | Cooking Time: 30 minutes | Servings: 100

Ingredients
- Black Pepper - ½ tsp
- Fresh Green Chives - 1 tsp
- Salt - 2 ¼ tsp
- Minced Pork - 1 lb.
- Chopped Cabbage - 1 lb.
- Lemon Grass - 1 tsp
- Chopped Ginger - 1 tbsp.
- Toasted Coriander Seeds - 2 tsp
- Minced Shallots - 1 tbsp.
- Lime Zest - 1 tsp
- Round Dumpling Wrappers - 100

Preparation
1. Take cabbage and add salt to it. Squeeze to drain out all the excessive liquid. Sauté minced pork for 5-10 minutes in a nonstick pan.
2. Now add squeezed cabbage and all other Ingredients in a bowl. Mix everything by using your hands.
3. Take dumpling wrappers and fill with 1 tbsp. of filling and seal them appropriately.
4. Transfer dumplings on steaming tray and add it in to your pot and close the lid.
5. Steam them for 15 – 20 minutes. Serve them hot with any of your favorite dip.

Nutritional Facts
Calories: 2430 | Carbohydrates: 49g | Protein: 223g | Fat: 175g | Fiber: 11g | Cholesterol: 101mg | Sugar: 13g | Sodium: 5700mg

6.2 Pork Dumplings

Preparation Time: 45 minutes | Cooking Time: 300 minutes | Servings: 100

Ingredients
- Whished Egg - 1
- Garlic - 4 cloves
- Chopped Ginger - 1 tbsp.
- Minced Pork - 1 ¾ lb.
- Sesame Oil - 3 tbsp.
- Shredded Cabbage - 5 cups
- Onion (Chopped) - 2 tbsp.
- Soy Sauce - 4 tbsp.
- Wonton Wrappers - 10

Preparation
1. Firstly, sauté the pork into the pan.
2. Take a bowl and mix up all Ingredients into the pork. Stir until well mixed.
3. Place the wonton wrapper on the flour and add 1 tsp of fillings unto the wonton wrapper.
4. Wet the edges of wonton wrappers with water and seal them.
5. Place dumplings in a covered steamer and steam for about 15-20 minutes.
6. Serve it hot.

Nutritional Facts
Calories: 2329 | Carbohydrates: 37.4g | Protein: 218.4g | Fat: 169g | Fiber: 10g | Cholesterol: 929.4mg | Sugar: 19g | Sodium: 5683mg

6.3 Chinese Pork Dumplings

Preparation Time: 35 minutes | Cooking Time: 20 minutes | Servings: 50

Ingredients
- Garlic - 3 cloves
- Soy Sauce - 2 tbsp.
- Egg Beaten - 1
- Sesame Oil - 1 ½ tbsp.
- Ground Pork - 1 lb.
- Vegetable Oil - for frying
- Ginger - 1 tbsp.
- Chopped Chives - 2 tbsp.
- Dumpling Wrappers - 50

Preparation
1. At first cook pork in a skillet.
2. Now mix pork, ginger, soy sauce, egg, sesame oil, ginger and garlic chives in a bowl.
3. Place a dumpling wrapper on a smooth work surface and add 1tbsp of the filling and crimp the edges.
4. Pour vegetable oil into the pan and fry dumplings.
5. Serve them hot.

Nutritional Facts
Calories: 2129 | Carbohydrates: 27.4g | Protein: 208.4g | Fat: 159g | Fiber: 9g | Cholesterol: 729.4mg | Sugar: 13g | Sodium: 4783mg

6.4 Garlic Chives and Pork Gyoza

Preparation Time: 45 minutes | Cooking Time: 25 minutes | Servings: 4

Ingredients
- Ginger - ½ inch piece
- Black Pepper - ¼ tsp
- Salt - ¼ tsp
- Soy Sauce - 2 tbsp.
- Egg Yolk - 1

- Cornstarch - ½ tbsp.
- Green chives - ¼ cup
- Garlic clove – 1
- Minced Pork - 0.5 lb.
- Gyoza Wrap – 4

Preparation
1. Combine all the Ingredients using your hands until they mix equally and add cooked pork into it
2. Place a small amount of filling in the center of the gyoza and close the ends of wrapper.
3. Steam for 10-15 minutes.
4. Serve hot with dumpling sauces.
5. Garnish with extra chopped chives.

Nutritional Facts
Calories: 1391 | Carbohydrates: 21g | Protein: 118g | Fat: 139g | Fiber: 5.7g | Cholesterol: 594mg | Sugar: 17g | Sodium: 3901mg

6.5 Steamed Pork Wontons

Preparation Time: 45 minutes | Cooking Time: 25 minutes | Servings: 60

Ingredients
- Kosher Salt - 1tbsp
- Mushrooms - 8
- Fresh Ginger - ½ tbsp.
- Garlic cloves - 2
- Mirin - 1 tbsp.
- Sesame oil - 1 tsp
- Black Pepper - 1/8 tsp
- Corn Starch - 1 tbsp.
- Soy sauce - 1 tbsp.
- Chili Pepper - 3
- Egg White - 1
- Scallions - 8
- Cabbage - 3 cups
- Pork – Small Cuts - 1 lb.
- Wonton Wraps - 60

Preparation
1. Grill small pork cuts on a grilling pan for 10 minutes.
2. Take a large bowl and add all the ingredient and mix them properly.
3. Take another bowl and dip cabbage into salty water. After 15 minutes remove all the excessive water.
4. Now incorporate all the Ingredients into a large bowl.
5. Fill wonton wraps and seal by brushing egg white on the end of edges.
6. Steam dumplings for 10-15 minutes. Serve with dipping sauces.

Nutritional Facts

Calories: 2301 | Carbohydrates: 27.4g | Protein: 211g | Fat: 161g | Fiber: 9g | Cholesterol: 909mg | Sugar: 11g | Sodium: 5101mg

6.6 Asian Steamed Dumplings

Preparation Time: 35 minutes | Cooking Time: 25 minutes | Servings: 60

Ingredients

- Wonton Wrappers - 60 pieces
- Sesame oil - 1tsp
- Pork chopped – 1 lb.
- Black Pepper – 1/8 tsp
- Soy Sauce - 1tbsp
- Chopped Onions - 2 tbsp.
- Garlic - 2 cloves
- Fresh Ginger - ½ tbsp.

Preparation

1. Mix all the Ingredients very well and add steamed pork into it.
2. Put a small amount of filling in the center of the wrapper. Wet your finger and moist the edges of the wrapper.
3. Place the dumplings on baking sheet and bake it for 10-15 minutes.
4. Ready to serve it with a sauce of your choice.

Nutritional Facts

Calories: 1350 | Carbohydrates: 78g | Protein: 127g | Fat: 115g | Fiber: 5g | Cholesterol: 535mg | Sugar: 4g | Sodium: 1760mg

6.7 Steamed Chinese Gyoza

- Preparation Time: 45 minutes | Cooking Time: 15 minutes | Servings: 50

Ingredients

- Onions - 3
- Canola oil - 2tbsp
- Garlic cloves - 2
- Chopped ginger - 1tbsp
- Soy sauce - ½ tbsp.
- Minced pork - ½ lb.
- Chopped cabbage - 4 cups
- Sesame oil - 1 tsp
- Gyoza - 50

Preparation

1. Sauté the cabbage with 1tbsp canola oil. After it transfer the cabbage to a large bowl.
2. Cut down all the Ingredients and add them into the sautéed cabbage.
3. Now, massage the mixture with your hands.
4. After it add 1tsp of the mixture into the middle of the wrapper.

5. Fold the edges of the wrapper Let the gyoza steam in the skillet for 1-2 minutes.
6. Remove the lid and let the gyoza. Cook for one more minute.
7. Serve it with hot sauce.

Nutritional Facts: Calories: 1929 | Carbohydrates: 19g | Protein: 199g | Fat: 141g | Fiber: 7g |Cholesterol: 621mg | Sugar: 11g | Sodium: 3983mg

6.8 Korean Pork Mandu

Preparation Time: 45 minutes | Cooking Time:15 minutes | Servings: 24

Ingredients
- Grated Cabbage - 1 Cup
- Sesame Oil - 2 tbsp.
- Chopped Onion - ½ Cup
- Minced Pork - ½ lb.
- Garlic - 1 tsp
- Ginger - 1 tsp
- Bean thread noodles - 1 cup
- Water – ½ cup
- Vegetable Oil (For Frying - 2-4 tbsp.
- Sesame Seeds - ¼ cup
- Chopped Mushrooms - 2 large
- Egg - 1 large
- Wonton Wrappers - 24
- Chopped Carrots - ½ Cup
- Scallions - ¼ Cup

Preparation
1. Cook the pork until brown and shred it. Add all the Ingredients and cook for about 5-8 minutes.
2. Place wonton wrappers on a flat surface. Add 1 tbsp. of the material in the center of the wrappers. Moist the ends of the wrappers with egg white and water.
3. Heat 2 tbsp. oil into skillet. Add wontons to hot oil add cook for about 2 minutes.
4. It's ready to serve.

Nutritional Facts
Calories: 2378 | Carbohydrates: 31g | Protein: 219g | Fat: 167g | Fiber: 11g |Cholesterol: 824mg | Sugar: 19g | Sodium: 4183mg

6.9 Pork Wontons

Preparation Time: 40 minutes | Cooking Time: 10 minutes | Servings: 30

Ingredients
- Grated ginger - 1 tsp
- Sesame oil - 2 tsp
- Sugar - 1 tsp
- Egg - 1
- Cornstarch - 1 tsp
- Minced Pork - ½ lb.
- Rice Wine - 1 tbsp.
- Yellow Chive - 3 tbsp.
- White Pepper - ¼ tsp
- Soy Sauce - 2 tsp
- Salt - ¼ tsp
- Wonton Wrappers - 30

Preparation
1. First cook the pork in the pan.
2. In a medium bowl combine minced pork, Chives, Wine, Ginger, Soy Sauce, Sesame Oil, Pepper, Salt, and Sugar. Mix all of them using a fork.
3. Now mix it in cornstarch thoroughly. Add beaten egg in the mixture.
4. Bring a large pot of water to a rolling boil.
5. Drop wontons into the pot and cook for about 5-6 minutes.
6. Remove wontons and stain them with a strainer to remove excessive oil.
7. Serve it with dipping sauce and garnish with scallions.

Nutritional Facts
Calories: 2129 | Carbohydrates: 129g | Protein: 208.4g | Fat: 159g | Fiber: 9.4g | Cholesterol: 529.4mg | Sugar: 11g | Sodium: 4091mg

6.10 Pan Fried Pork Buns

Preparation Time: 45 minutes | Cooking Time: 10 minutes | Servings: 50

Ingredients
- Sugar - 1 tsp
- Lukewarm Water - 140ml
- Yeast - 1 tsp
- Minced Pork - 250g
- Spring Onion - 2tbsp
- Soy Sauce - 2tsp
- Rice Wine - ½ tsp
- Ginger - ½ tbsp.
- Salt - ¼ tsp

- Sesame oil - ½ tsp
- Canola oil - 1 tbsp.
- Sesame Seeds - ¼ cup
- Sugar - 1 tsp

Preparation
1. Put all the Ingredients for the filling into a bowl. Meanwhile cook minced pork for 5 minutes and add spices.
2. Combine all ingredient and fill dough in the enter. Close dough in a round shape bun.
3. Heat up oil in the pan over high heat stir fry until they turn golden brown.
4. Sprinkle sesame seeds and spring onion over and cook for another 30 seconds.
5. Ready to serve crispy buns.

Nutritional Facts
Calories: 2100 | Carbohydrates: 27g | Protein: 209g | Fat: 149g | Fiber: 9g | Cholesterol: 729mg | Sugar: 13g | Sodium: 4183mg

6.11 Soup Dumplings (Xiao Long Bao)

Preparation Time: 45 minutes | Cooking Time: 15 minutes | Servings: 30

Ingredients
- Sugar - ¾ tsp
- Minced Pork - 1 lb.
- White Pepper - 1 Pinch
- Sesame Oil - ½ tsp
- Ginger - 1 tbsp.
- Rice wine - 2 tbsp.
- Soy Sauce - 3 tsp
- Salt - ¾ tsp
- Water - 3 tbsp.
- Diced aspic - ½ Inch Pieces

Preparation
1. Take the minced pork and cook it in a pan for 5-7 minutes. In a bowl add pork and all Ingredients except aspic.
2. Combine everything well for about 2 minutes. Gently fold the diced aspic.
3. Place 1 tbsp. of filling in the center of each bao.
4. Using metal steamer boil water and steam bao over high heat for 8 minutes.
5. Now serve it with the sauce of your choice.

Nutritional Facts
Calories: 1909| Carbohydrates: 19g | Protein: 189g | Fat: 141g | Fiber: 5g | Cholesterol: 629mg | Sugar: 11g | Sodium: 3733mg

6.12 Char Siu barbeque Pork

Preparation Time: 45 minutes | Cooking Time: 20 minutes | Servings: 30

Ingredients
- Brown Sugar – 1/3 cup
- Soy Sauce - ½ cup
- Honey- 1/3 cup
- Pork Tenderloins - 2
- Red Food Color - 2 tbsp.
- Rice Wine - ¼ cup
- Ketchup - 1/3 cup
- Hoisin Sauce - 2 tbsp.
- Chicken Spice Powder - 1 tsp

Preparation
1. Cook the pork in a skillet for 5 minutes.
2. In a saucepan, combine all ingredients and cook over medium-low heat.
3. Stir the ingredients until they are thoroughly mixed. Take the dish off the stove and let it cool for a few minutes.
4. Fill Ingredients in the wontons and steam for about 15 minutes.
5. Serve with marinara sauce.

Nutritional Facts
Calories: 1759| Carbohydrates: 15g | Protein: 177g | Fat: 130g | Fiber: 3.7g |Cholesterol: 553mg | Sugar: 10.3g | Sodium: 2913mg

6.13 Chestnut Pork Dumplings

Preparation Time: 35 minutes | Cooking Time: 20 minutes | Servings: 30

Ingredients
- Soy sauce - 1 tbsp.
- Minced Pork - 1 lb.
- Grated ginger - 2 tsp
- Rice wine vinegar - 2 tsp
- Sesame oil - 1 tbsp.
- Chopped Chestnuts - 1 cup
- Cornstarch - 2 tbsp.
- Sugar - 2 tsp
- Black pepper - ½ tsp
- Salt - 1 tsp
- Dumpling wrappers - 30

Preparation
1. Firstly, cook the minced pork for few minutes. Remove from heat and add all Ingredients and seasonings.
2. Place dumpling wrapper in your palm and fill with stuffing. Carefully seal your wrapper.

3. Steam them for 15 minutes in a steamer and serve with dipping sauce of your choice.

Nutritional Facts
Calories: 1909 | Carbohydrates: 19g | Protein: 179g | Fat: 109g | Fiber: 5g | Cholesterol: 595mg | Sugar: 13g | Sodium: 3183mg

6.14 Pork and Tea Leave Wontons

Preparation Time: 25 minutes | Cooking Time: 20 minutes | Servings: 12

Ingredients
- Pork Minced - 1 cup
- Oolong tea leaves - 2 tbsp.
- Green Chilies - ¼ cup
- Spring Onions - 1 chopped
- Ginger - 1 tsp
- Garlic clove - 1
- Soy Sauce - 1 tbsp.
- Oil - 3 tbsp.
- Water - ½ cup
- Salt - 1 tsp
- Dumpling wrappers - 12

Preparation
1. Cook pork with salt for 3-5 minutes.
2. Steep tea in water for 2-3 minutes and separate tea leaves.
3. Combine tea leaves, pork and all the other remaining Ingredients.
4. Fill dumpling wrappers and stir fry them for 10 minutes.
5. Serve with mint sauce.

Nutritional Facts
Calories: 1349 | Carbohydrates: 13g | Protein: 157g | Fat: 97g | Fiber: 3.3g | Cholesterol: 343mg | Sugar: 13g | Sodium: 2486mg

6.15 Pepper Stuffed Dumplings

Preparation Time: 35 minutes | Cooking Time: 10 minutes | Servings: 12

Ingredients
- Chopped bell pepper - ¼ cup
- Rice cooked - ¼ cup
- Onions - ¼ cup
- Zucchini - ¼ cup
- Cumin powder - 1 tsp
- Oil - 1 cup
- Ground pork - ½ cup
- Dumpling wrappers - 12

Preparation
1. In a pan, heat oil and pour grounded, zucchini, onion and bell pepper.
2. When meat is cooked remove them from heat. Add all the remaining Ingredients and mix well.
3. Fill dumpling wrappers and pinch edges to close.
4. Deep fry in oil for 5-7 minutes until turned crispy
5. Serve with marinara sauce.

Nutritional Facts
Calories: 2309 | Carbohydrates: 27g | Protein: 211g | Fat: 149g | Fiber: 9g | Cholesterol: 657mg | Sugar: 13g | Sodium: 4783mg

6.16 Apple and Maple Pork Dumplings

Preparation Time: 35 minutes | Cooking Time: 10 minutes | Servings: 12

Ingredients
- Chopped Pork - 1 cup
- Apple Cider Vinegar - 1 tbsp.
- Apple (Chopped) - 1
- Maple Syrup - 2 tbsp.
- Spicy Mustard - 1 tsp
- Salt - 1 tsp
- Bread Crumbs - 2 tbsp.
- Oil - ½ cup
- Dumplings Wrappers - 12

Preparation
1. Cook pork for 5 minutes until juicy and tender.
2. Combine all Ingredients in a bowl and add pork along with them.
3. Fill Ingredients in dumpling wrappers and seal them.
4. Stir fry for 3 minutes and squeeze lime juice for topping.

Nutritional Facts
Calories: 1999 | Carbohydrates: 21g | Protein: 191g | Fat: 139g | Fiber: 11g | Cholesterol: 710mg | Sugar: 13g | Sodium: 4321mg

6.17 Chopped Pork and Herb Stuffed Dumplings

Preparation Time: 35 minutes | Cooking Time: 10 minutes | Servings: 12

Ingredients
- Minced Pork - ½ cup
- Orange Juice - 2 tbsp.
- Rosemary - 2 tsp
- Sage - 1 tsp
- Chicken Broth - ½ cup
- Salt - ½ tsp
- Garlic Clove - 1
- Ginger Slices - 1 tbsp.

- Sun Dried Tomatoes - ¼ cup
- Stuffing Crumbs - ½ cup
- Oil - ¼ cup
- Dumpling Wrappers - 12

Preparation
1. Stir fry minced pork for few minutes then add orange juice, rosemary, ginger, garlic, salt, chicken broth and sun dried tomatoes.
2. Bring them to boil and pour stuffing crumbs. Mix all Ingredients and turn off flame.
3. Fill dumpling wrappers and press to close their edges.
4. Stir fry for 3-5 minutes until they are golden in color.
5. Serve with lemon and chili sauce.

Nutritional Facts
Calories: 1991 | Carbohydrates: 29g | Protein: 197g | Fat: 149g | Fiber: 9g | Cholesterol: 878mg | Sugar: 14g | Sodium: 4103mg

6.18 Fancy Pork Dumplings

Preparation Time: 25 minutes | Cooking Time: 10 minutes | Servings: 12

Ingredients
- Cooked Pork - ½ cup
- Green Onions - ¼ cup
- Lemon Juice - 1 tbsp.
- Parmesan Cheese - ¼ cup
- Doenjiang - 1 tbsp.
- Gochujang - 1 tbsp.
- Melted Butter - ½ cup
- Garlic Clove (Pressed) - ½ cup
- Salt - ½ tsp
- Italian Seasonings - 1 tbsp.
- Oil - 3 tbsp.
- Dumpling Wrappers - 12

Preparation
1. Mix all Ingredients evenly in a large bowl using hands.
2. Scoop 1 tbsp. of filling and place in center of dumpling wrapper. Seal them carefully.
3. Fry for 3 minutes and serve with chili sauce.

Nutritional Facts
Calories: 2091 | Carbohydrates: 31g | Protein: 204g | Fat: 169g | Fiber: 11g | Cholesterol: 729.4mg | Sugar: 19g | Sodium: 3793mg

7 SEAFOOD AND FISH DUMPLINGS

7.1 Fish & Shrimp Dumplings

Preparation Time: 35 minutes | Cooking Time: 15 minutes | Servings: 36

Ingredients
- shelled shrimps - 6 oz.
- white fish (finely chopped) - 6 oz.
- carrots (finely sliced) - 2 large
- ginger (grated) - 1tbsp
- sesame oil - 1tsp
- rice wine - 1tbsp
- soy sauce (light) – 1 tbsp.
- Cornstarch - 1tbsp
- white pepper - pinch
- red chili - pinch
- sea salt - pinch
- mushrooms (finely diced) - 3-4
- scallions or garlic chives - 3-6
- wonton wrappers - 36

Preparation
1. Add all Ingredients and toss until mixed together.
2. Place the wonton wrappers on a clean surface and add 1tbsp of filling, use thumb and forefingers to seal.
3. Take a large sized skillet fill it with around 1 inch of water. Place the dumplings and sliced carrots in a bamboo steamer and cover the lid. Steam them until wrappers become translucent.
4. Serve the dumplings and sliced carrots warm in a nice platter.

Nutritional Facts

Calories: 943 | Carbohydrates: 96.3g | Protein: 114.6g | Fat: 11.1g | Fiber: 3.5g | Cholesterol: 70mg | Sugar: 3g | Sodium: 2509mg

7.2 Shrimp Green Curry Dumplings

Preparation Time: 35 minutes | Cooking Time: 15 minutes | Servings: 15

Ingredients
- deveined & shelled shrimps - 24 small
- scallions (chopped) - ½ cup
- cilantro (chopped) - ½ cup
- sesame oil - 1tsp
- Salt - ½ tsp
- coconut milk (full-fat) – 2 tbsp.
- green curry paste - 2 tsp
- Serrano pepper (chopped) - 2 tsp
- round dumpling wrappers - 15

Preparation
1. Add shrimp, coconut milk, green curry paste and salt to food processor and give it a few rounds till all Ingredients are well combined. Shift the mixture into a bowl and add all other Ingredients.
2. Take the wonton wrappers and add a teaspoon full of the filling. Fold them by rubbing water on each of the edges of wrappers and make folds by the use of your thumb and forefingers.
3. Take a large sized skillet fill it with ½ inch water. Heat it till the water comes to boil. Place the dumplings in a bamboo steamer and cover the lid. Steam them until the filling is cooked completely.
4. Serve the dumplings warm.

Nutritional Facts
Calories: 778 | Carbohydrates: 88.4g | Protein: 984.4g | Fat: 9.6g | Fiber: 3g |Cholesterol: 35mg | Sugar: 3g| Sodium: 2412mg

7.3 Pork & Shrimp Dumplings

Preparation Time: 35 minutes | Cooking Time: 15 minutes | Servings: 15

Ingredients
- pork (ground) - 1 lb.
- shelled shrimps - lb.
- soy sauce - 3 tbsp.
- sesame oil - 3 tbsp.
- garlic cloves (chopped) – 5
- green onions (chopped)   - 4
- ginger (grated) - 3 tbsp.
- egg whites - 4
- lemon juice - 1
- water chestnuts (canned) - 4 oz.
- black pepper (freshly ground) - ½ tsp
- kosher salt - ½ tsp
- wonton wrappers - 15

Preparation
1. Add all Ingredients except water chestnuts into a food processor and make a chunky mixture, then add water chestnuts to it and fold them into the mixture.
2. Prepare all the dumplings using the filling mixture, steam them using a bamboo steamer and serve while hot.

Nutritional Facts
Calories: 931 | Carbohydrates: 99g | Protein: 117g | Fat: 19g | Fiber: 5g | Cholesterol: 75mg | Sugar: 2.3g | Sodium: 2590mg

7.4 Tiger Prawn Dumplings

Preparation Time: 35 minutes | Cooking Time: 15 minutes | Servings: 10

Ingredients
- shelled & diced tiger prawns - 4 oz.
- pork(ground) - 4 oz.
- ginger(grated) – 1 tbsp.
- green spring onions (chopped) - 2
- rice wine - 1 tbsp.
- sesame oil - 1 tsp
- soy sauce – 1 tbsp.
- sea salt - pinch
- black pepper (freshly ground) - pinch
- Cornstarch - 2 tsp
- wonton wrappers - 10

Preparation
1. Add all Ingredients into a bowl and mix until well combined.
2. Prepare all the dumplings using the filling mixture, by placing around 1-2 teaspoons of the mixture in a wrapper, fold the sides around the mixture leaving the top open.
3. Steam them using a bamboo steamer and serve while hot.

Nutritional Facts
Calories: 1143 | Carbohydrates: 105g | Protein: 124g | Fat: 21g | Fiber: 3.7g | Cholesterol: 97mg | Sugar: 3.5g | Sodium: 3019mg

7.5 Golden Dumplings

Preparation Time: 35 minutes | Cooking Time: 15 minutes | Servings: 30

Ingredients
- Pork (ground) - 12 oz.
- diced prawns (minced) - 12oz
- soy sauce - 1 tbsp.
- Shao sing rice wine - 1 tbsp.
- rice vinegar - 1 tbsp.
- sesame oil - 1 tsp
- Cornstarch - 1 tbsp.

- ginger(grated) - 1 tbsp.
- Sugar - pinch
- sea salt - pinch
- scallions (finely chopped) - 3
- garlic cloves (finely chopped) - 5
- red fresh chili - 1 medium
- wonton wrappers - 30
- vegetable oil - for frying

Preparation
1. Add all Ingredients in a large sized bowl and toss until finely mixed together.
2. Place the wonton wrappers on a clean surface or dish and top each wrapper in the middle with a spoon full of filling. Fold them by rubbing water on each of the edges of wrappers and make folds by the use of your thumb and forefingers.
3. Fry the dumplings in vegetable oil until golden brown color appears for around 3-4 minutes, place them on tissue paper or paper towel to drain the excess oil.
4. Serve the dumplings warm in a nice platter.

Nutritional Facts
Calories: 955 | Carbohydrates: 86g | Protein: 99.4g | Fat: 10.1g | Fiber: 3g | Cholesterol: 67mg | Sugar: 3g | Sodium: 219mg

7.6 Sea Scallop Dumplings

Preparation Time: 35 minutes | Cooking Time: 15 minutes | Servings: 50

Ingredients
- Shrimps-finely chopped - ½ pound
- crab meat-chopped - ½ pound
- sea scallops-chopped - ½ pound
- ginger (minced) - 1 tbsp.
- Chives - ¼ cup
- soy sauce - 2 tsp
- Shao sing rice wine - 1 tbsp.
- white pepper - pinch
- Sugar - 1 tsp
- egg white - 1
- round dumpling wrappers - 50

Preparation
1. Add scallops and shrimp to a food processor and give it a few rounds to form paste.
2. Add all Ingredients, including the paste, into a bowl and mix until well combined.
3. Prepare all the dumplings using the filling mixture, by placing around 1-2 teaspoons of the mixture in a wrapper, fold the sides making pleats.
4. Steam them using a bamboo steamer and serve while hot.

Nutritional Facts: Calories: 1073 | Carbohydrates: 103g | Protein: 117g | Fat: 17g | Fiber: 3.5g | Cholesterol: 71mg | Sugar: 5g | Sodium: 2179mg

7.7 Shrimp & Hoisin Sauce Dumplings

Preparation Time: 35 minutes | Cooking Time: 10 minutes | Servings: 12

Ingredients

- Shrimps (finely chopped) - ½ cup
- chicken broth - 1 tbsp.
- pork(ground) - ½ cup
- mushroom (finely chopped) - ¾ cup
- celery(chopped) - ¼ cup
- cilantro(chopped) – 2 tbsp.
- carrots (finely chopped) - ¾ cup
- peanuts(crushed) - ¼ cup
- hoisin sauce - 1 tsp
- brown sugar - 1 tsp
- dumpling wrappers - 12
- vegetable oil - for frying

Preparation

1. Add all Ingredients into a bowl and mix until well combined.
2. Whisk chicken broth and cornstarch together and add to the mixture, mix all the Ingredients.
3. Prepare the dumplings using the filling mixture, by placing around 1-2 teaspoons of the mixture in a wrapper, fold the wrapper into half then fold its sides by using fingers making pleats.
4. Steam them using a bamboo steamer or fry them in hot oil until golden brown and serve while hot with Chinese chili sauce.

Nutritional Facts

Calories: 1091 | Carbohydrates: 101g | Protein: 119g | Fat: 17g | Fiber: 2.7g | Cholesterol: 70mg | Sugar: 2.3g | Sodium: 2134mg

7.8 Lobster Dumplings

Preparation Time: 35 minutes | Cooking Time: 10 minutes | Servings: 12

Ingredients

- lobster meat-cooked - ½ cup
- parmesan cheese - ¼ cup
- bread crumbs - ½ cup
- butter (melted) - ½ cup
- Salt - pinch
- green onions (chopped) - 2
- garlic cloves (crushed) - 2
- lemon juice of 1 lemon
- Italian seasoning - 1 tbsp.
- dumpling wrappers - 12
- Oil - for frying

Preparation
1. In a bowl add Italian seasoning butter, salt and garlic, use it as sauce or pour over the prepared dumplings.
2. Mix all other Ingredients make a chunky mixture.
3. Prepare all the dumplings by adding 1-2 teaspoon full of the filling mixture into the wrappers and then closing them by forming folds on the sides using fingers.
4. Fry the dumplings in hot oil.

Nutritional Facts: Calories: 793 | Carbohydrates: 77g | Protein: 97g | Fat: 9.9g | Fiber: 1.7g |Cholesterol: 57mg | Sugar: 1.3g | Sodium: 1909mg

7.9 Spicy Salmon Dumplings

Preparation Time: 35 minutes | Cooking Time: 15 minutes | Servings: 12

Ingredients
- smoked salmon (chopped) - ½ cup
- bread crumbs - ¼ cup
- bell pepper (chopped) - ¼ cup
- Red chili pepper - 5
- Celery (chopped) - ¼ cup
- Egg - 1
- Garlic (pressed) - 2
- Onion (chopped) - ¾ cup
- lemon juice of 1 lemon
- Cumin - 1 tsp
- Oil - 3 tbsp.
- dumpling wrappers - 12

Preparation
1. Add 1tbsp oil, cumin, salt, garlic lemon juice and peppers in a blender. Blend all ad make sauce.
2. In pan heat oil, add celery, bell peppers and onion and sauté, then add salmon and cook for 2-4 min. Add egg and whisk.
3. Remove heat and add prepared sauce and breadcrumbs to mixture.
4. Prepare dumplings using the mixture, by placing around 1-2 teaspoons of the mixture in a wrapper, fold the wrapper into half then fold its sides by using fingers making pleats.
5. Steam them using a bamboo steamer and serve hot.

Nutritional Facts
Calories: 953 | Carbohydrates: 96.3g | Protein: 117g | Fat: 13g | Fiber: 3.7g |Cholesterol: 69mg | Sugar: 3.1g | Sodium: 2319mg

7.10 Ricotta Cheese & Fish Dumplings

Preparation Time: 35 minutes | Cooking Time: 10 minutes | Servings: 12

Ingredients
- garlic powder – 1 tsp
- white fish (finely chopped) – 4 oz.

- ricotta cheese - 8 oz.
- mozzarella cheese - ½ cup
- onion powder - 1 tsp
- Italian seasoning - 1 tbsp.
- marinara sauce - 1 cup
- dumpling wrappers - 12
- Oil - for frying

Preparation
1. Add all Ingredients into a bowl and mix until well combined.
2. Prepare all the dumplings using the filling mixture, by placing around 1-2 teaspoons of the mixture in a wrapper, fold the sides using water on fingers forming pleats.
3. Deep fry the dumplings in hot oil until golden brown.
4. Serve hot with marinara sauce.

Nutritional Facts
Calories: 898 | Carbohydrates: 86g | Protein: 98g | Fat: 9g | Fiber: 2.3g | Cholesterol: 48mg | Sugar: 2.1g | Sodium: 2148mg

7.11 Turkey - Shrimp and Cranberry Sauce Dumplings

Preparation Time: 35 minutes | Cooking Time: 10 minutes | Servings: 10

Ingredients
- diced shrimps - 6 oz.
- Turkey meat (chopped) - 1 cup
- Cranberry sauce - 1 tbsp.
- Mashed potatoes - ½ cup
- Garlic cloves (crushed) - 2
- Green onions (chopped) - 2
- Dumpling wrappers - 10
- Oil - for frying

Methods
1. Mix all Ingredients in a bowl until thoroughly mixed.
2. Prepare the dumplings using the filling, by placing 1-2 teaspoons of the mixture in a wrapper, fold the sides.
3. Fry the dumplings till golden brown in heated oil.
4. Serve hot with Thai chili sauce.

Nutritional Facts
Calories: 1031 | Carbohydrates: 99g | Protein: 121g | Fat: 19g | Fiber: 3g | Cholesterol: 73mg | Sugar: 3g | Sodium: 2101mg

7.12 Tuna Cheese Dumplings

Preparation Time: 35 minutes | Cooking Time: 15 minutes | Servings: 10

Ingredients

- Tuna - 1 can
- Parmesan cheese - 1 tbsp.
- Pickle relish - 2 tbsp.
- Mayonnaise - ½ cup
- Celery (chopped) - 1 tbsp.
- Onion (chopped) - 1 tbsp.
- Lemon juice 1 lemon
- Dumpling wrappers - 10

Preparation

1. Add all Ingredients into a bowl and mix until well combined.
2. Prepare all the dumplings using the filling mixture, by placing around 1-2 teaspoons of the mixture in a wrapper, fold the sides.
3. Steam them using a bamboo steamer and serve while hot.

Nutritional Facts: Calories: 743 | Carbohydrates: 87g | Protein: 103g | Fat: 10.3g | Fiber: 3.5g | Cholesterol: 39mg | Sugar: 2.1g | Sodium: 2017mg

7.13 Lemon Shrimp Dumplings

Preparation Time: 35 minutes | Cooking Time: 10 minutes | Servings: 12

Ingredients

- deveined & diced shrimp - 1 cup
- Butter - 2 tbsp.
- garlic cloves (crushed) - 2
- onion (chopped) - ¾ cup
- mushrooms (chopped) - ¾ cup
- Cream - ¾ cup
- lemon juice 1 lemon
- Salt - pinch
- Flour – 1 tsp
- parmesan cheese - ¼ cup
- fresh parsley (chopped) - 1 tbsp.
- Dumpling wrappers - 12
- Oil - for frying

Preparation

1. Heat butter in a wok, add flour and heat until light brown color appears, add cream and let it simmer.
2. Add shrimp, cheese and other Ingredients gradually, let the mixture cool down.
3. Prepare all the dumplings using the filling mixture, by placing around 1-2 teaspoons of the mixture in a wrapper, fold the sides by using water on fingers.

4. Fry them until golden brown, serve hot with chili sauce.

Nutritional Facts
Calories: 990 | Carbohydrates: 97g | Protein: 117g | Fat: 13g | Fiber: 3.9g | Cholesterol: 71mg | Sugar: 4.8g | Sodium: 2886mg

7.14 Broccoli & Prawn Dumplings

Preparation Time: 35 minutes | Cooking Time: 10 minutes | Servings: 10

Ingredients
- diced tiger prawns - 4 oz.
- broccoli (steamed & chopped) - ½ cup
- Milk - 2 tbsp.
- cheddar cheese (shredded) - ¼ cup
- garlic powder - 1 tsp
- dumpling wrappers - 10
- Oil - for frying

Preparation
1. Add all Ingredients into a bowl and mix until well combined.
2. Prepare all the dumplings using the filling mixture, by placing around 1-2 teaspoons of the mixture in a wrapper, fold the sides around the mixture leaving the top open.
3. Fry the dumplings until golden brown and serve while hot.

Nutritional Facts
Calories: 773 | Carbohydrates: 93g | Protein: 101.3g | Fat: 11g | Fiber: 3g | Cholesterol: 57mg | Sugar: 2.1g | Sodium: 2148mg

7.15 Creamy White Fish Dumplings

Preparation Time: 35 minutes | Cooking Time: 15 minutes | Servings: 12

Ingredients
- white fish (cooked & flakey) - 1 cup
- garlic cloves - 2
- onion (chopped) - ½ cup
- Cumin - 1 tsp
- Cilantro (chopped) - ½ cup
- Jalapeno (chopped) - 1
- Cream - ¼ cup
- lemon juice of 1 lemon
- dumpling wrappers - 12
- Salsa - for dip

Preparation
1. Add all Ingredients into a bowl and mix until well combined.
2. Prepare all the dumplings using the filling mixture, by placing around 1-2 teaspoons of the mixture in a wrapper, fold the sides around the mixture leaving the top open.

3. Take a large sized skillet fill it with around 1 inch of water. Heat it till the water comes to boil. Place the dumplings and sliced carrots in a bamboo steamer and cover the lid. Steam them until the filling is cooked completely and the wrappers become translucent.
4. Serve with salsa sauce while hot.

Nutritional Facts

Calories: 1037 | Carbohydrates: 98g | Protein: 119g | Fat: 17g | Fiber: 4.2g | Cholesterol: 69mg | Sugar: 3g | Sodium: 2790mg

7.16 Fish & Beans Dumplings

Preparation Time: 35 minutes | Cooking Time: 15 minutes | Servings: 12

Ingredients

- Tuna fish - 6 oz.
- Cannellini beans (boiled) - ½ cup
- Garlic cloves (crushed) - 2
- Scallions (chopped) - 2
- Black pepper - 1 tsp
- Red chili flakes - 1 tsp
- Salt - 1 tsp
- Lemon juice – 2 tbsp.
- Oil - 2 tbsp.
- Dumpling wrappers - 12

Preparation

1. Add oil in a wok, sauté fish with garlic and scallions, then add beans, add spices and cook for 2-3 min.
2. Let the mixture cool.
3. Add it to a food processor and give it a few rounds, until beans turn to flakey mixture.
4. Fill the wrappers with the mixture, and steam it in a bamboo steamer.
5. Serve with chili sauce.

Nutritional Facts

Calories: 919 | Carbohydrates: 91g | Protein: 101g | Fat: 9g | Fiber: 3.3g | Cholesterol: 57mg | Sugar: 2.8g | Sodium: 2399mg

7.17 Crunchy Prawn Dumplings

Preparation Time: 35 minutes | Cooking Time: 10 minutes | Servings: 12

Ingredients
- Crawfish - 1 cup
- Creole seasoning – 1 tbsp.
- Mushrooms - ¼ cup
- Flour - ½ cup
- Onion (chopped) - ¼ cup
- garlic cloves (chopped) - 3
- Eggs - 2
- Oil - for frying
- dumpling wrappers - 12

Preparation
1. Whisk eggs in a bowl, dip prawns in eggs then in flour and repeat.
2. Deep fry the prawns until golden brown.
3. Add 1tbsp oil in wok, sauté onions and garlic then add mushrooms Creole seasoning and prawns. Mix well and set aside to cool down.
4. Add 1-2 teaspoons of mixture in wrappers and fry the dumplings till golden brown.
5. Serve with sauce.

Nutritional Facts
Calories: 873 | Carbohydrates: 89g | Protein: 87g | Fat: 11g | Fiber: 3g | Cholesterol: 55mg | Sugar: 3.3g | Sodium: 2397mg

7.18 Sweet Crab Dumplings

Preparation Time: 25 minutes | Cooking Time: 10 minutes | Servings: 10

Ingredients
- crab meat (chopped) - ¼ cup
- cream cheese - 4 oz.
- Honey - 1 tbsp.
- Milk - ¼ cup
- dumpling wrappers - 10
- Oil - for frying

Preparation
1. Add all Ingredients into a bowl and mix well.
2. Prepare all the dumplings using the mixture, by placing a teaspoon of mixture in a wrapper, fold the sides.
3. Heat oil in a pan, cook dumplings on both sides until golden color appears, place them on paper towel to let absorb extra oil.

Nutritional Facts Calories: 675 | Carbohydrates: 79g | Protein: 99g | Fat: 9g | Fiber: 4.3g | Cholesterol: 59mg | Sugar: 1.7g | Sodium: 2103mg

7.19 Fish Cake Dumplings

Preparation Time: 35 minutes | Cooking Time: 20 minutes | Servings: 12

Ingredients
- sea bass or any white fish - 1 cup
- garlic cloves (crushed) - 1
- cilantro (chopped) - ¼ cup
- green onion (chopped) - 1
- lemon juice of 1 lemon
- Breadcrumbs - ½ cup
- Salt - pinch
- Pepper - pinch
- Egg - 1
- white rice (boiled) - ½ cup
- Oil - 2 tbsp.
- wonton wrappers - 12

Preparation
1. Add oil in a wok, add garlic, onion, cilantro sauté well, then add fish, cook for 2 to 5 min.
2. Add egg, scramble it with fish then add rice and all other Ingredients
3. Prepare all the dumplings using the filling, in the wrappers, fold the sides around the mixture leaving the top open.
4. Steam them using a bamboo steamer and serve with tartar sauce.

Nutritional Facts
Calories: 997 | Carbohydrates: 91g | Protein: 109g | Fat: 11.1g | Fiber: 3.3g | Cholesterol: 67mg | Sugar: 3g | Sodium: 2110mg

7.20 Spicy Shrimp Dumplings

Preparation Time: 45 minutes | Cooking Time: 17 minutes | Servings: 15

Ingredients
- shelled & diced shrimps - 1 cup
- garlic cloves (pressed) - 2
- onion (chopped) - ¼ cup
- ginger (grated) - 1 tsp
- jalapeno (chopped) – 1
- Cumin - 1 tsp
- lemon juice of 1 lemon
- Pepper - pinch
- Salt - pinch
- Oil – 2 tbsp.
- wonton wrappers - 15

Preparation
1. Add oil in wok, sauté all Ingredients then add shrimps and cook for 2 to 5min.

2. Place the wonton wrappers on a dish and top each wrapper in the middle with a teaspoon full of the filling. Fold them by rubbing water on each of the edges of wrappers and make folds by the use of your thumb and forefingers.
3. Take a large sized skillet fill it with ½ inch water. Heat it till the water comes to boil. Place the dumplings in a bamboo steamer and cover the lid. Steam them until the filling is cooked completely. Serve the dumplings warm.

Nutritional Facts
Calories: 1099 | Carbohydrates: 98.1g | Protein: 120g | Fat: 17g | Fiber: 3g | Cholesterol: 79mg | Sugar: 4.1g | Sodium: 2709mg

8 POULTRY DUMPLINGS

8.1 Soup Dumplings

Preparation Time: 30 minutes | Cooking Time: 15 minutes | Servings: 30

Ingredients
- Chicken Stock - 6 cups
- White Wine/ Apple Cider - ½ cups
- Carrots - 2
- Garlic - 3
- Honey - 2 tsp
- Peppercorns - 5 whole
- Bay Leaves - 2
- Chicken - 3 lb.
- Onion - 1
- Celery Ribs - 2
- Canola Oil - 2 tbsp.
- Black Pepper - ½ tsp
  FOR SOUP
- Fresh Parsley - 2 tsp
- Whipping Cream - ½ cup
- Salt - ¼ tsp
- Pepper - ¼ tsp
- Fresh Thyme - 2 tsp

Preparation
1. Take carrots, celery, onions, garlic and sauté them for 6 minutes. Add bay leaves, sugar and wine to sautéed vegetables.
2. Boil and shred chicken and mix all above Ingredients.
3. Fill dumplings with 1 tbsp. of mixture and carefully shape them in half. Boil for 5 minutes.
4. For Soup, mix and stir all Ingredients and pour on dumplings. Enjoy!Serve them sizzling hot.

Nutritional Facts
Calories: 696 | Carbohydrates: 57g | Protein: 25g | Fat: 22g | Fiber: 9g | Cholesterol: 55mg | Sugar: 18g | Sodium: 1710mg

8.2 Traditional Chicken Dumplings

Preparation Time: 30 minutes | Cooking Time: 15 minutes | Servings: 30

Ingredients
- Salt - ¼ tsp
- Soy sauce - 1 tbsp.
- Chicken minced - 1 cup
- Bell Pepper - 1 tsp
- Black Pepper - ½ tsp

- Spring Onions - ¼ cup
- Canola Oil - ½ tbsp.
- Ginger Garlic Paste - ½ tbsp.

Preparation

1. Take a skillet, add canola oil and give medium heat. Put minced chicken and ginger garlic paste, cook for 10 minutes.
2. Add salt, black pepper, soy sauce, spring onions and bell peppers.
3. Mash all Ingredients together and fill wonton wraps with 1 tbsp of mixture.
4. Pan fry wontons in a nonstick skillet over medium to high heat.
5. Wontons ready to serve.

Nutritional Facts

Calories: 329 | Carbohydrates: 39g | Protein: 10g | Fat: 32g | Fiber: 2g | Cholesterol: 1.5mg | Sugar: 13g | Sodium: 1679mg

8.3 Green Chili Chicken Momos

Preparation Time: 25 minutes | Cooking Time: 20 minutes | Servings: 30

Ingredients

- Chicken - 200 g
- Onions - 1
- Ginger - 1 tsp
- Black Pepper - ½ tsp
- Vinegar - 1 tsp
- Green Chilies - 2
- Soy Sauce - 2 tsp
- Butter - 2 tsp
- Canola oil - 2 tsp

Preparation

1. Boil chicken and shred them into ½ inch slices.
2. Sauté ginger, onions and green chilies in butter.
3. Sprinkle black pepper, vinegar and soy sauce in vegetables and chicken.
4. Fill momos dough with 1 tbsp. filling and accurately close edges.
5. Let momos to steam for about 7-8 minutes and serve with any of your favorite sauce.

Nutritional Facts

Calories: 398 | Carbohydrates: 34g | Protein: 19g | Fat: 21g | Fiber: 4g | Cholesterol: 14mg | Sugar: 3g | Sodium: 2343mg

8.4 Chicken Jiaozi

Preparation Time: 25 minutes | Cooking Time: 20 minutes | Servings: 30

Ingredients

- Chicken Breasts - 1 lb.
- Onions - 2
- Ginger - 2 inch

- Garlic cloves - 3
- Soy Sauce - 2 tsp
- Salt - ½ tsp
- Pepper - ½ tsp
- Spring onions - ¼ cup

Preparation
1. Put chicken, ginger garlic, salt, pepper and soy sauce in a chopper.
2. Mince them finely.
3. Add spring onions in minced mixture.
4. Take Jiaozi wraps and fill them with them 1 tbsp. of mince in each wrap.
5. Let them simmer for 15 minutes and they are ready to eat.

Nutritional Facts
Calories: 440 | Carbohydrates: 45g | Protein: 40g | Fat: 27g | Fiber: 3g | Cholesterol: 35mg | Sugar: 6g | Sodium: 2189mg

8.5 Celery Stalk and Chicken Broth Dumplings

Preparation Time: 25 minutes | Cooking Time: 20 minutes | Servings: 30

Ingredients
- Carrots - 2 medium
- Water - 2 quarts
- Celery stalks - 2
- Whole Chicken - 3 lb.
- Kosher Salt - 2 tsp
- Black Pepper - ½ tsp
- Vegetable Shortening - 3 tbsp.
- Fresh chives - ¼ cup

Preparation
1. Put carrots, chicken, celery stalks, salt, black pepper and water in a big cooker.
2. Let them simmer for about 1 hour under medium to low heat.
3. Separate chicken from broth and remove all the bones and shred into small slices.
4. Place chicken shreds in the broth.
5. Meanwhile, prepare dough to 1-inch thick and pinch in 1 ½ inch pieces.
6. Place these pieces into your broth and cook for about 8-10 minutes until you get your desired consistency.
7. Put freshly chopped chives on top and dish out attractively.

Nutritional Facts
Calories: 390 | Carbohydrates: 31g | Protein: 13g | Fat: 17g | Fiber: 2.5g | Cholesterol: 13mg | Sugar: 2g | Sodium: 3379mg

8.6 One Pot Soup Dumplings

Preparation Time: 25 minutes | Cooking Time: 20 minutes | Servings: 30

Ingredients
- Celery - 1 stalk
- Onion Chopped - ½ cup
- Minced Garlic - 1 tsp
- Chicken thighs - 5 lbs.
- Butter - 2 tbsp.
- Water - 4 cups
- Dried thyme - ½ tsp
- Dried parsley - 1 tsp
- Bay Leaf - 1
- Ground pepper - ½ tsp
- Salt - 1 tsp
- All Purpose Flour - 3 tbsp.
- Olive Oil - 2 tbsp.

Preparation
1. Heat olive oil and butter in a stockpot, add chicken on medium flame until golden brown.
2. Now add salt, pepper, bay leaf, garlic, onion, celery, thyme and parsley to stockpot and let them simmer for 2 hours on medium heat.
3. Remove bones from thighs meat and add meat again in the pot.
4. Take all purpose flour and add water in it, stir well. Pour this mixture into your pot.
5. On other hand, prepare a sticky dough.
6. Pour the dough by the help of teaspoon in the pot along with the broth.
7. Steam them for about 10 minutes and serve.

Nutritional Facts
Calories: 859 | Carbohydrates: 43g | Protein: 53g | Fat: 51g | Fiber: 5g | Cholesterol: 19mg | Sugar: 7g | Sodium: 2769mg

8.7 Cream Cheese Sriracha Sauce Wontons

Preparation Time: 35 minutes | Cooking Time: 15 minutes | Servings: 30

Ingredients
- Minced Chicken - 1 lb.
- Sesame Oil - ¼ tsp
- Green Onions - 2 pieces
- Honey - 3 tbsp.
- Cream Cheese - 250 g
- Soy Sauce - 2 tbsp.
- Sriracha Sauce - 1 tbsp.
- Salt - ½ tsp
- Vegetable oil - ½ cup

- Egg - 1

Preparation
1. Place minced chicken in a skillet cook for 5 minutes.
2. Chop green onions.
3. Pour sesame oil, green onions, honey, cream cheese, soy sauce, Sriracha sauce and salt in the minced chicken and knead to combine all Ingredients.
4. Take wonton dough and fill the mixture.
5. Pour vegetable oil in nonstick pan and heat the oil on medium to high heat.
6. Put your wonton in the oil and fry them until they turn crispy golden.
7. Serve them with any sauce or simply with a soy sauce.
8. Bon Appetite!

Nutritional Facts
Calories: 572 | Carbohydrates: 47g | Protein: 16g | Fat: 25g | Fiber: 1g | Cholesterol: 16mg | Sugar: 1.2g | Sodium: 1771mg

8.8 Schezwan Chicken Bao

Preparation Time: 15 minutes | Cooking Time: 35 minutes | Servings: 30

Ingredients
- Warm Water - ¼ cup
- Sugar - 1 tsp
- Yeast - ½ tsp
- All Purpose Flour - 1 cup
- Salt - ½ tsp
- Oil - 3 tsp
- Ginger Garlic Paste - 1 tsp
- Minced Chicken - ½ lb.
- Chopped Onions - ½ cup
- Schezwan Sauce - 2 tsp
- Soy Sauce - 1 tsp

Preparation
1. Combine warm water, yeast and sugar. Stir them and keep it aside.
2. Add all purpose flour and knead evenly. Divide dough into 4 parts.
3. In a pan, add oil and ginger garlic paste. Sauté them and then add chopped onions and minced chicken. Cook them for 5-7 minutes and pour soy sauce and schezwan sauce and keep it aside.
4. Roll dough into 4 circles and fill them with maximum filling. Close to form bao buns.
5. Steam bao buns with 20-25 minutes and serve with mint or chili sauce.

Nutritional Facts
Calories: 959 | Carbohydrates: 76g | Protein: 37g | Fat: 22g | Fiber: 5g | Cholesterol: 11mg | Sugar: 3g | Sodium: 1759mg

8.9 Rice Ball Dumplings

Preparation Time: 30 minutes | Cooking Time: 15 minutes | Servings: 12

Ingredients
- Minced Chicken – ½ lb
- Chinese Spice powder – 1tbsp
- Mirin - 2tbsp
- Soy Sauce - 3tbsp
- Ginger - 2tbsp
- Sake - 2 tbsp.
- Sushi Rice - 1 cup
- Brown Sugar - ½ tbsp.
- Salt - ¼ tsp
- Rice Vinegar - 1/8 cup
- Sesame Seeds - ½ cup
- Cilantro - ¼ cup

Preparation
1. Boil chicken, ginger, mirin, soy sauce and Chinese spices until all liquid is evaporated.
2. Now add remaining Ingredients and mix them well.
3. Take sushi rice and shaped into round patty. Fill mixture in the middle and close to form a round ball.
4. Served with coated sesame seeds and garnish with chives.

Nutritional Facts
Calories: 1212 | Carbohydrates: 14g | Protein: 54g | Fat: 49.3g | Fiber: 12.1g | Cholesterol: 16mg | Sugar: 17g | Sodium: 2030mg

8.10 Chicken Fajita Wontons

Preparation Time: 25 minutes | Cooking Time: 20 minutes | Servings: 12

Ingredients
- Salt - ½ tsp
- Cumin - ½ tsp
- Chili Powder - 2 tsp
- Garlic Minced - 1 tsp
- Minced Chicken - 1 Cup
- Cheese - 1 Cup
- Onion - ¼ Cup
- Cayenne Pepper - ¼ tsp
- Oil - 2 tsp
- Wonton Wraps - 12

Preparation
1. Sauté minced chicken with garlic, salt, chili powder, onion, and cumin.
2. Add cayenne pepper and cheese to the chicken.
3. Take wonton wraps and fill them evenly. Pinch edges to seal.
4. Stir fry wonton for 5-10 minutes and serve with cheese sauce.

Nutritional Facts
Calories: 786 | Carbohydrates: 94g | Protein: 38g | Fat: 39g | Fiber: 9.3g | Cholesterol: 45mg | Sugar: 13g | Sodium: 2390mg

8.11 Sicilian Chicken Dumplings

Preparation Time: 30 minutes | Cooking Time: 15 minutes | Servings: 12

Ingredients
- Grounded Chicken - 1 Cup
- Red Wine - ¼ Cup
- Oregano - ¼ tbsp.
- Basil - ¼ tbsp.
- Black Pepper - ½ tbsp.
- Parsley - ½ tbsp.
- Cayenne Pepper - ¼ tbsp.
- Fennel Seeds - ¼ tbsp.
- Salt - 1 tsp
- Paprika - ½ tbsp.
- Oil - 3 tbsp.
- Dumpling Wrappers - 12

Preparation
1. Mix all the Ingredients and place in refrigerator for about 1 hour.
2. After that fill in the dumpling wrappers with 1 tbsp. of mixture.
3. Deep fry dumplings for at least 3 minutes from each side until well cooked.

4. Serve with guacamole.

Nutritional Facts
Calories: 1213 | Carbohydrates: 13g | Protein: 59g | Fat: 50.3g | Fiber: 11.1g | Cholesterol: 17mg | Sugar: 5g | Sodium: 4930mg

8.12 Zucchini Stuffed Wontons

Preparation Time: 30 minutes | Cooking Time: 15 minutes | Servings: 12

Ingredients
- Zucchini - ¼ Cup
- Bell Pepper - ¼ Cup
- Onion - ¼ Cup
- Cumin - 1 tsp
- Minced Chicken - ½ Cup
- Cooked Rice - ¼ Cup
- Salt - ½ tsp
- Oil - 3 tbsp.
- Wonton Wraps - 12

Preparation
1. Sauté chicken with onion, Salt, Zucchini, Bell Pepper, and Cumin.
2. Remove from heat and add cooked rice. Use your hands to mix evenly.
3. Fill wonton wraps and stir fry them for 5-7 minutes.
4. Serve with marinara sauce.
5. Garnish with chopped spring onions on top.

Nutritional Facts
Calories: 986 | Carbohydrates: 19g | Protein: 48g | Fat: 49g | Fiber: 10.3g | Cholesterol: 15mg | Sugar: 13g | Sodium: 2410mg

8.13 Sweet and Tangy Chicken Momos

Preparation Time: 30 minutes | Cooking Time: 15 minutes | Servings: 12

Ingredients
- Chopped Chicken Breast - 1 Cup
- Bell Pepper - ¼ Cup
- Onion - ¼ Cup
- Carrot - ¼ Cup
- Chopped Pineapple - ¼ Cup
- Pineapple Juice - 4 tbsp.
- Oil - 3 tsp
- Momo Wraps - 12

Preparation
1. Cook chicken and all vegetables until they are tender.
2. Add pineapple juice and mix equally.
3. Fill momo wraps and carefully seal them.

4. Stir fry momo for 3 minutes until they turn brown.
5. Serve with any sweet and sour sauce.

Nutritional Facts
Calories: 1186 | Carbohydrates: 99g | Protein: 28g | Fat: 29g | Fiber: 7.3g | Cholesterol: 39mg | Sugar: 19g | Sodium: 2101mg

8.14 Curry Chicken Wonton

Preparation Time: 30 minutes | Cooking Time: 15 minutes | Servings: 12

Ingredients
- Curry Powder - 1 tbsp.
- Chopped Chicken Breast - 1 Cup
- Coconut Milk - 1 Cup
- Chopped Potatoes - 1 Large
- Chopped Onions - ¼ Cup
- Oil - 3 tbsp.
- Wonton Wraps - 12

Preparation
1. Cook coconut oil in the pan and gently whisk in a curry powder. Bring sauce to a boil.
2. In another pan, Boil chicken, Onion, and Potatoes for 3-5 minutes. Drain all the liquid.
3. Add 2 tbsp. of curry sauce to the chicken and mix them equally.
4. Fill the mixture in the wonton wrappers and pinch-seal them.
5. Stir fry in oil for 3 minutes and serve wontons with curry sauce.

Nutritional Facts Calories: 1268 | Carbohydrates: 14g | Protein: 48g | Fat: 39g | Fiber: 9.3g | Cholesterol: 45mg | Sugar: 13g | Sodium: 2309mg

8.15 Chicken Bbq Momos

Preparation Time: 30 minutes | Cooking Time: 15 minutes | Servings: 12

Ingredients
- Ground Chicken - 1 Cup
- Smoked Cheese Shreds - ½ Cup
- BBQ Sauce - 2 tbsp.
- Onion - ¼ Cup
- Garlic Chives - 3 tbsp.
- Oil - 3 tbsp.

Preparation
1. Pour Chicken in a pan and cook for few minutes until tender.
2. Add cheese, BBQ sauce, and chopped onions. Gently mix all Ingredients.
3. Take the dough and roll it over to make a circle. Put the mixture in the center and close it to form a round dough.
4. Stir fry momos for 5 minutes and serve with BBQ sauce.
5. Garnish with chopped garlic chives.

Nutritional Facts: Calories: 1176 | Carbohydrates: 19g | Protein: 41g | Fat: 75g | Fiber: 5g | Cholesterol: 25mg | Sugar: 2.1g | Sodium: 2200mg

8.16 Creamy Chicken Gyoza

Preparation Time: 30 minutes | Cooking Time: 15 minutes | Servings: 12

Ingredients
- Chopped Chicken - 1 Cup
- Cream of Chicken Soup - 1 Can
- Chopped Mushrooms - ¼ Cup
- Chopped Onions - ¼ Cup
- Milk - ¼ Cup
- Italian Seasonings - 1 tbsp.
- Garlic Powder - 1 tbsp.
- Onion Powder - 1 tbsp.
- Oil - 2 tbsp.
- Gyoza Wraps - 12

Preparation
1. Combine onion and mushrooms and cook for few minutes. Add chicken and cook until tender.
2. For the sauce add spices, Milk, and Soup. Bring them to a boil.
3. Add 2 tbsp. of sauce in the chicken and mix evenly.
4. Fill the mixture in gyoza wrappers and seal them carefully.
5. Stir fry in oil for 3 minutes and serve with creamy sauce.

Nutritional Facts
Calories: 1213| Carbohydrates: 35g | Protein: 57g | Fat: 49.3g | Fiber: 11.1g |Cholesterol: 27mg | Sugar: 5.1g | Sodium: 3930mg

8.17 Leftover Chicken Dumplings

Preparation Time: 35 minutes | Cooking Time: 5 minutes | Servings: 12

Ingredients
- Leftover Stuffing - ½ Cup
- Leftover Chicken Gravy - 2 tbsp.
- Cranberry Sauce - 1 tbsp.
- Mashed Potatoes - ½ Cup
- Oil - 2 tbsp.
- Cook Chicken - 1 Cup
- Dumpling Wrappers - 12

Preparation
1. Combine all Ingredients in a bowl and mix everything using your hands.
2. Fill in dumplings wrapper and seal them carefully.
3. Stir fry dumplings for 3-5 minutes.
4. Serve with cranberry sauce.

Nutritional Facts
Calories: 1347 | Carbohydrates: 13g | Protein: 69g | Fat: 27g | Fiber: 7.9g |Cholesterol: 15mg | Sugar: 4.3g | Sodium: 3100mg

8.18 Bok Choy Wonton Soup

Preparation Time: 15 minutes | Cooking Time: 35 minutes | Servings: 12

Ingredients
- Chopped Garlic - 1 tsp
- Bok Choy - ½ Cup
- Chicken Broth - 10 Cups
- Green Onions - 4
- Oil - 1 tbsp.
- Mushrooms - ½ Cup
- Chopped Ginger - 1 tbsp.
- Wonton Wraps - 12

Preparation
1. Put oil in a nonstick pan and sauté ginger and garlic for 1 minute.
2. Add chicken broth and green onions, bring them to boil.
3. Let broth simmer for 20 minutes and add bok choy and mushrooms. Cook for another 3 minutes.
4. Pour prefilled wontons and let them cook for 5-7 minutes until they float on surface.
5. Serve them hot.

Nutritional Facts
Calories: 1670 | Carbohydrates: 21g | Protein: 77g | Fat: 19g | Fiber: 9.5g | Cholesterol: 17mg | Sugar: 3.8g | Sodium: 3301mg

8.19 Air Fried Chicken Mandu

Preparation Time: 25 minutes | Cooking Time: 15 minutes | Servings: 12

Ingredients
- Chicken - 1 Cup
- Chopped Onion - ¼ Cup
- Bell Pepper - ¼ Cup
- Mustard Sauce - 3 tbsp
- Zucchini - ¼ Cup
- Broccoli - ¼ Cup
- Salt - ½ tsp
- BBQ Sauce - 2 tbsp

Preparation
1. Cook chicken, Onions, Zucchini, and Bell Peppers initial tender and juicy. Add salt, BBQ sauce, and mustard. Mix gently.
2. Fill the dough of dumplings and air fry them for 15 minutes over 200°C temperature.
3. Serve with leftover BBQ sauce.

Nutritional Facts
Calories: 1343 | Carbohydrates: 35g | Protein: 62g | Fat: 39g | Fiber: 5.1g | Cholesterol: 15mg | Sugar: 6.3g | Sodium: 2196mg

8.20 Apple and Chicken Dumplings

Preparation Time: 40 minutes | Cooking Time: 5 minutes | Servings: 12

Ingredients
- Cooked Chicken - 1 Cup
- Cheese Shred - ½ Cup
- Sliced Apple - ½ Cup
- Oil - 3 tbsp
- Dumpling Wrappers - 12

Preparation
1. Finally Chopped Chicken, Cheese and apples. Mix everything evenly.
2. Take dumplings wrappers and fill in the Ingredients.
3. Stir fry for 5 minutes until golden brown from each side.
4. Serve with sweet and tangy sauce.

Nutritional Facts
Calories: 1241 | Carbohydrates: 23g | Protein: 55g | Fat: 27g | Fiber: 3.9g | Cholesterol: 13.3mg | Sugar: 4.5g | Sodium: 2978mg

9 SWEET DUMPLINGS

9.1 Crispy Cherry Cheese Wontons

Preparation Time: 35 minutes | Cooking Time: 18 minutes | Servings: 12

Ingredients
- Canned Cherry Pie – ¼ cup
- Whipping Cream - 2 tbsp
- Vanilla Extract - 5 drops
- Cinnamon Powder - ½ tsp
- Water - 1 tsp
- Egg - 1
- Sugar - 3 tbsp
- Cream Cheese - 4oz
- Wonton Wraps - 12

Preparation
1. Beat whipping cream until its fluffy.
2. In other bowl add cream cheese and sugar and start beating.
3. Add vanilla extract in the mixture and beat for few more minutes.
4. Whisk egg and water and keep it aside.
5. Meanwhile pre heat oven to 190 °C.
6. Combine whipping cream and cream cheese mix together.
7. Take wonton wraps add 1 tbsp of cream mix and ½ tsp of cherry pie filling.
8. Fold wontons into a triangular shape and brush with egg mix.
9. Sprinkle cinnamon on top.
10. Bake for 18 minutes until wontons turn crispy.
11. Serve with chocolate dip.

Nutritional Facts
Calories: 742 | Carbohydrates: 50.4g | Protein: 14.4g | Fat: 54g | Fiber: 2.1g | Cholesterol: 330.5mg | Sugar: 4.7g | Sodium: 464mg

9.2 Traditional Pennsylvania Apple Dumplings

Preparation Time: 1 hour | Cooking Time: 40 minutes | Servings: 25

Ingredients
For Dough
- Small Apple - 7
- Butter - 6 tbsp
- Brown Sugar - 1 cup
- Cinnamon - ¾ tsp
- Nutmeg – ⅛ tsp
- Lemon Zest - 1 tsp
- Pie Crust - 9 inches   7

For Sauce
- Corn Starch - 8 tbsp
- Butter - 6 tbsp
- Sugar - 1 cup
- Water - 2 cups
- Lemon Zest - 1 tbsp
- Lemon Juice - 3 tbsp

Preparation
1. Wash and peal apple and empty them from inside.
2. Combine butter, sugar, lemon zest and all spices, stir them well and fill in apples.
3. Place a baking dish and spray with butter, preheat oven to 190 °C.
4. Take pie crust and place apple in the middle. Fold all the crust over the apple and make a square shape. Bake for 40 minutes.
5. For sauce, combine cornstarch, sugar and water bring to boil until it becomes thick.
6. Remove from heat and add butter, lemon juice and zest. Stir and pour sauce on apple pie crust.

Nutritional Facts
Calories: 990 | Carbohydrates: 67g | Protein: 12g | Fat: 15g | Fiber: 5g | Cholesterol: 379mg | Sugar: 5.9g | Sodium: 679mg

9.3 Raspberry Peach Dumplings

Preparation Time: 1 hour | Cooking Time: 25 minutes | Servings: 4

Ingredients
- Cinnamon - 1 tsp
- Sugar - ¼ cup
- Butter - 2 tbsp
- Pie Crush – 4 pieces/9 inches
- Peaches - 2
- Egg - 1
- FOR SAUCE
- Raspberries - 60 oz
- Water - $^{11}/_2$ tbsp
  - Sugar - 2 tbsp
- Lemon Juice - 1 tsp

Preparation
1. Place a pan in the oven and grease with cooking spray.
2. Preheat oven to 204 °C.
3. Peel and cut the peaches into 2 halves.
4. Combine, sugar, cinnamon and melted butter, whisk together.
5. Take a pie dough and roll to make a 13-inch circle. Cut each circle in half.
6. In each semi-circle place a half peach and 1/4 tsp of butter mixture.
7. Fold your semi-circle and seal edges and brush egg on top.
8. Place it in the oven and bake for 25 minutes.

9. Meanwhile, combine all sauce Ingredients and blend them together.
10. Strain all the liquid and pour on the baked dumplings.
11. Ready to dig.

Nutritional Facts

Calories: 735 | Carbohydrates: 49g | Protein: 13.5g | Fat: 45g | Fiber: 3.5g | Cholesterol: 351mg | Sugar: 11g | Sodium: 438mg

9.4 Sweet Maillenknödel Dumplings

Preparation Time: 45 minutes | Cooking Time: 15 minutes | Servings: 15

Ingredients

For Dough

- Butter - 1 tbsp
- Salt - ½ tsp
- Milk - 25 ml
- All Purpose Flour - 150 g
- Egg Yolks - 2

Filling Ingredients

- Butter - ¼ cup
- Bread Crumbs - 1 cup
- Apricot - 12 small

Preparation

1. Heat butter in a pot and pour milk and salt. Bring it to boil.
2. Add this liquid in the flour and keep stirring until everything comes together. Keep dough aside to cool down.
3. After it cools add egg yolks and knead continuously. Make long sausage of dough.
4. Make mall pieces of dough and flatten them in a circle.
5. Place an apricot in the center and close to form round shape dumplings.
6. Boil dumplings until they float on water.
7. In a pan, heat butter and breadcrumbs. Pour boiled dumplings in them and coat boiled dumplings in these crumbs.
8. Delicious dessert is ready!

Nutritional Facts

Calories: 864 | Carbohydrates: 71g | Protein: 17.8g | Fat: 59g | Fiber: 4.7g | Cholesterol: 390mg | Sugar: 13.9g | Sodium: 530mg

9.5 Spice Pumpkin Treat

Preparation Time: 25| Cooking Time: 35 minutes | Servings: 10

Ingredients

- Crescent Dough Roll - 1
- Pumpkin Puree - 1 cup
- Butter - ½ cup
- Water - 1 cup
- Cinnamon Spice - 1 tbsp
- Vanilla Ice cream - 1 litre
- Brown Sugar - 1 tbsp
- Cornstarch - 2 tbsp

Preparation

1. In a bowl combine cornstarch, butter, brown sugar and cinnamon. Stir them to well.
2. In microwave, melt butter, water and sugar mixture.
3. Combine pumpkin puree and cornstarch mixture.
4. Take crescent roll and add 2 tbsp. of pumpkin mix. Start rolling the crescent from wide side. Place them in a baking dish.
5. Pour butter mixture over all the rolls in the baking dish. Bake for 35 minutes over 177°C, sauce will become thick.
6. Serve one roll with 1 scoop of vanilla ice cream and enjoy.

Nutritional Facts

Calories: 640 | Carbohydrates: 39g | Protein: 11g | Fat: 25g | Fiber: 2g | Cholesterol: 279mg | Sugar: 3g | Sodium: 371mg

9.6 Awameh Dumplings

Preparation Time: 30 minutes | Cooking Time: 15 minutes | Servings: 15

Ingredients

- Flour - 2 cups
- Instant Yeast - 2 tsp
- Water - 2 cups
- Sugar - 2 tsp
- Oil - for Frying
- Cornstarch - 1 tbsp

Syrup

- Water - 1 cup
- Lemon Juice - 1 tsp
- Rose Water - 1 tsp
- Sugar - 1 cup

Preparation

1. Combine water, yeast, flour and cornstarch. Mix well and let it to rest for 1 hour, cover with warm towel.
2. After an hour, knead dough again and make small balls.
3. In a pot, heat oil over medium to high heat.
4. Pour balls and deep fry until they float above oil.
5. For syrup mix sugar, rose water, water, lemon juice, and give it a boil.
6. Pour Awameh balls in the syrup, serve them hot.

Nutritional Facts
Calories: 924 | Carbohydrates: 30g | Protein: 12g | Fat: 65g | Fiber: 5g | Cholesterol: 505mg | Sugar: 21g | Sodium: 701mg

9.7 Strawberry Knödel

Preparation Time: 25 minutes | Cooking Time: 15 minutes | Servings: 12

Ingredients
- Strawberries - 12
- Breadcrumbs - 1 cup
- Butter - ½ cup
- Sugar Icing - 2 tbsp

Preparation
1. Make a knÖdel dough using instructions.
2. Cut them in small pieces and roll to make a circle.
3. Place a strawberry in the center of the circle and close them to form a ball.
4. Pour them in a boiling water for 7-10 minutes and take them out using a strainer.
5. In a nonstick pan, heat butter and add breadcrumbs. Sauté crumbs for 2-3 minutes.
6. Add boiled knÖdel in the butter mix pan and stir them to coat breadcrumbs evenly.
7. Sprinkle icing sugar and on top and serve.

Nutritional Facts
Calories: 347 | Carbohydrates: 25g | Protein: 8g | Fat: 33g | Fiber: 5.9g | Cholesterol: 115mg | Sugar: 13g | Sodium: 121mg

9.8 Sweet Cinnamon Banana Wontons

Preparation Time: 25 minutes | Cooking Time: 10 minutes | Servings: 15

Ingredients
- Cinnamon - 3 tbsp
- Sugar - 2 tsp
- Ripe Banana - 1 large
- Unsalted Butter - 2 tbsp
- Melted Dark Chocolate - 2 oz

Preparation
1. In a bowl mash sugar, banana and cinnamon.
2. Take your wraps and fill with banana mixture. Carefully seal wontons.
3. Heat butter first and pan fry wontons until they are turned golden brown.

4. Served wontons with melted butter on top.

Nutritional Facts
Calories: 540 | Carbohydrates: 29g | Protein: 9g | Fat: 39g | Fiber: 4.3g | Cholesterol: 205mg | Sugar: 23g | Sodium: 290mg

9.9 Sweet Vegan Tropical Dumplings

Preparation Time: 40 minutes | Cooking Time: 5 minutes | Servings: 6

Ingredients
- Peppa Pig Water - 1 cup
- Agar Agar Powder - 1 tbsp
- Butter Pea Flower Tea - 1
- Mango - ½ cup
- Kiwi - 3
- Strawberries - 3

Preparation
1. Boil water and add agar agar powder. Keep boiling until it starts to thicken.
2. Pour this liquid in a plate and let it cool on room temperature for 25 minutes.
3. Meanwhile, cut all fruits in small cubes.
4. Take a cookie cutter and cut the liquid that is now turned into a transparent wrap.
5. Fill the wrap with all fruits and fold them in a crescent shape.
6. Serve them fresh.

Nutritional Facts
Calories: 549 | Carbohydrates: 23g | Protein: 12g | Fat: 7g | Fiber: 6.9g | Cholesterol: 57mg | Sugar: 11g | Sodium: 77mg

9.10 Glutinous Rice Dumplings

Preparation Time: 35 minutes | Cooking Time: 10 minutes | Servings: 15

Ingredients
- Sesame Seeds – Black - 100 g
- Butter Unsalted - 65 g
- Sugar - 90 g

  Dough
- Boiled water - 110 ml
- Cold Water - 100 ml
- Rice Flour - 2 cups

  Sweet Sauce
- Water - 5 cups
- Brown Sugar - 2 tbsp
- Ginger Slices - 4 (1 inch each)

Preparation
1. Roast sesame seeds for 5 minutes and let them cool. Meanwhile melt butter.
2. Blend sesame seeds, butter and sugar.
3. Knead to make a paste and divide it into 23 portions by making small balls.
4. For dough, mix glutinous rice flour and warm water. Big lumps will be formed.
5. Add cold water to remove lumps and knead for few minutes.
6. Make a long sausage and cut dough into 23 portions.
7. Take each portion and roll to make a circle, fill each with sesame paste.
8. Seal them in round shape and boil them for 2-4 minutes.
9. Take water, brown sugar and ginger slices. Bring everything to boil.
10. Pour sugar mix on boiled dumplings and dish out.

Nutritional Facts
Calories: 709 | Carbohydrates: 30g | Protein: 12g | Fat: 53g | Fiber: 3.9g | Cholesterol: 295mg | Sugar: 17g | Sodium: 234mg

9.11 Cream Cheese Apple Wontons

Preparation Time: 30 minutes | Cooking Time: 15 minutes | Servings: 30

Ingredients
- Apple Butter - ½ cup
- Cream Cheese - 1 cup
- Cinnamon Sugar - 2 tbsp
- Vegetable Oil - for Frying
- Wonton wraps - 50

Preparation
1. Finely whip apple butter and cream cheese.
2. Take wonton wraps and fill them with cheese filling.
3. Heat a skillet with vegetable oil and deep fry wonton wraps.
4. Sprinkle cinnamon sugar and serve them hot.

Nutritional Facts
Calories: 341 | Carbohydrates: 21g | Protein: 11g | Fat: 37g | Fiber: 5g | Cholesterol: 157mg | Sugar: 11g | Sodium: 187mg

9.12 Glazed Cinnamon Rice Ball

Preparation Time: 45 minutes | Cooking Time: 15 minutes | Servings: 30

Ingredients
- Golden Raisins - 49
- Cinnamon Tea - 1 cup
- Salt - 1 tsp
- Sweet Rice Flour - 2 cups
- Roasted Walnuts - ½ cup

Preparation
1. Take a bowl and add salt and sweet rice flour. Gradually add water and knead until a soft dough is formed.
2. Divide dough into 24 portions. Take each portion and roll into circle.
3. Add 2 raisins in the center of each ball and pour them in boiling water for 8 minutes or until they float above the surface.
4. Once they float above water, immediately transfer to ice cold water.
5. Top rice balls with roasted walnuts.

Nutritional Facts
Calories: 809 | Carbohydrates: 37g | Protein: 19g | Fat: 59g | Fiber: 5.9g | Cholesterol: 301mg | Sugar: 23g | Sodium: 335mg

10 DIPPING SAUCES

10.1 Peanut Butter Sauces

Preparation Time: 15 minutes | Cooking Time: 2 minutes | Servings: 15

Ingredients
- Oil - 2 tbsp
- Rice Vinegar - 1 tsp
- Soy Sauce - 2 tsp
- Fresh Ginger - 1 tbsp
- Tahini - 2 tbsp
- Honey - 1 tbsp
- Peanut Butter - 1 tbsp
- Vegetable Stock - ¼ cup

Preparation
1. Put all Ingredients in a bowl and stir them well.
2. Heat oil in a pan and add to your mixture.
3. Mix everything well and serve.

Nutritional Facts
Calories: 18 | Carbohydrates: 0.7g | Protein: 0.2g | Fat: 1.7g | Fiber: 0.3g | Cholesterol: 0mg | Sugar: 0.1g | Sodium: 171.4mg

10.2 Classic Chili Sauce

Preparation Time: 15 minutes | Cooking Time: 2 minutes | Servings: 30

Ingredients
- Ginger - ¼ cup
- Garlic - ¼ cup
- Sesame Seed - ¼ cup
- Chili Flakes - ¼ cup
- Canola Oil - 3 tbsp

Preparation
1. In a small bowl add ginger, garlic, sesame seeds and chili flakes.
2. Mix all Ingredients evenly.
3. Heat canola oil in a pan and gently pour the heated oil over the spices. Sauce is ready to serve.

Nutritional Facts
Calories: 863 | Carbohydrates: 21.7g | Protein: 15g | Fat: 79g | Fiber: 9.6g | Cholesterol: 0mg | Sugar: 3.5g | Sodium: 35mg

10.3 Tangy Chili Sauce

Preparation Time: 15 minutes | Cooking Time: 18 minutes | Servings: 15

Ingredients
- Tomato - 4

- Whole Dried Chili - 9
- Coriander - Half Bunch
- Water - 2 cups
- Ginger - 1 tsp
- Garlic - 2 tsp
- Onion - 3 tbsp
- Chili Paste - ½ cup
- Canola Oil - 1 tsp
- Vinegar - 3 tsp
- Salt - ½ tsp
- Ketchup - 2 tbsp
- Spring Onion - 3 tbsp

Preparation

1. Boil tomatoes, whole dried chilies and coriander in water for 1o minutes.
2. In a skillet, heat oil and add chopped ginger, garlic and onion and sauté for 2-3 minutes.
3. Add chili paste, salt, ketchup, vinegar and boiled mixture and cook until it forms a paste like texture.
4. Top it with spring onions and serve.

Nutritional Facts

Calories: 278 | Carbohydrates: 41.3g | Protein: 6.5g | Fat: 17g | Fiber: 9.5g |Cholesterol: 0mg | Sugar: 34g | Sodium: 1897mg

10.4 Doubanjiang Sauce

- Preparation Time: 15 minutes | Cooking Time: 0 minutes | Servings: 15

Ingredients

- Soy Sauce - 2 tbsp
- Brown Sugar - 1 tsp
- Sesame Seeds - 1 tsp
- Sesame Oil - 1 tsp
- Water - 3 tbsp
- Doubanjiang - ½ tsp
- Black Chinese Vinegar - 2 tsp
- Chili Crisp - 1 tsp
- Minced Garlic - 1 tsp
- Spring Onion - 3 tbsp
- Coriander Chopped - 3 tbsp

Preparation

1. Mix together all the above mentioned Ingredients in a bowl and stir them well.
2. Serve with the choice of your dumplings.

Nutritional Facts

Calories: 187 | Carbohydrates: 17.3g | Protein: 5g | Fat: 13.2g | Fiber: 1.1g |Cholesterol: 0mg | Sugar: 9.3g | Sodium: 2159mg

10.5 Traditional Garlic Dip

Preparation Time: 10 minutes | Cooking Time: 0 minutes | Servings: 15

Ingredients
- Garlic - 2 tbsp
- Black Vinegar - ½ cup
- Spring Onions - 3 tbs

Preparation
1. Take a bowl and mix garlic and black vinegar.
2. Top with spring onion and serve.

Nutritional Facts
Calories: 98| Carbohydrates: 12g | Protein: 5.9g | Fat: 0.1g | Fiber: 0.5g |Cholesterol: 0mg | Sugar: 0.3g| Sodium: 80.5mg

10.6 Crystal Red Sauce

Preparation Time: 13 minutes | Cooking Time: 2 minutes | Servings: 15

Ingredients
- Red Pepper - 1 tsp
- Carrot - 2 tsp
- Sugar - ¼ cup
- Salt - ½ tsp
- Vinegar-Red Vine - ½ cup

Preparation
1. Crush red pepper.
2. Wash and shred carrots.
3. Add all items in a bowl.
4. Bring them to boil and simmer for 3 minutes.
5. Set the pan on side and set it to cool.
6. Serve on room temperature.

Nutritional Facts
Calories: 45 | Carbohydrates: 6g | Protein: 0.2g | Fat: 0.1g | Fiber: 0.5g |Cholesterol: 0mg | Sugar: 5g | Sodium: 1975mg

10.7 Soy Sesame Sauce

Preparation Time: 10 minutes | Cooking Time: 0 minutes | Servings: 15

Ingredients
- Soy Sauce - 3 tbsp
- Rice Vinegar - 1 tbsp
- Chili Sauce – ½ tbsp
- Sesame Oil - 1 tbsp

Preparation
1. Take a container, add all Ingredients and combine them together.
2. Stir them and sauce is ready to serve.

Nutritional Facts Calories: 150 | Carbohydrates: 13g | Protein: 8g | Fat: 1.5g | Fiber: 3.5g |Cholesterol: 0mg | Sugar: 6.3g | Sodium: 189mg

10.8 Classic Soy Dip

Preparation Time: 15 minutes | Cooking Time: 0 minutes | Servings: 15

Ingredients

- Scallions - 5 tbsp (chopped)
- Soy Sauce - 2 tsp
- Black Chinese Vinegar - 2 tsp
- Garlic - 2 tsp (minced)
- Chili Oil - 1 tsp

Preparation

1. Stir fry scallions and garlic for 1 minute.
2. Combine all above ingredients and serve with your choice of dumplings.

Nutritional Facts
Calories: 253 | Carbohydrates: 21g | Protein: 13g | Fat: 2.1g | Fiber: 3.7g |Cholesterol: 0mg | Sugar: 8.1g | Sodium: 197mg

10.9 Honey and Apple Cider Dip

Preparation Time: 10 minutes | Cooking Time: 0 minutes | Servings: 10

Ingredients

- Apple Cider Vinegar - 2 tbsp
- Honey - 1 tbsp
- Soy Sauce - 1tsp
- Chili Oil - 1 tsp

Preparation

1. Mix and whisk all Ingredients and serve.

Nutritional Facts
Calories: 101 | Carbohydrates: 13g | Protein: 6g | Fat: 0.5g | Fiber: 1.5g |Cholesterol: 0mg | Sugar: 0.7g | Sodium: 191mg

10.10 Gluten Free Tamari Dip

Preparation Time: 15 minutes | Cooking Time: 0 minutes | Servings: 15

Ingredients

- Vegan Mayo - 1 tsp
- Dijon Mustard - 1 tsp
- Spirit Vinegar - 1 tsp
- Balsamic Vinegar - 1 tsp
- Cranberry Sauce - 2 tsp
- Tamari Soy Sauce (Gluten free) - 2 tsp
- Sriracha Sauce - 1 tsp
- Gluten Free Ketchup - 3 tbsp

Preparation
2. Take all Ingredients into a bowl and whisk them gradually until they are combined into a dip.
3. Serve with your favorite momo.

Nutritional Facts
Calories: 178 | Carbohydrates: 15.3g | Protein: 3.9g | Fat: 11.2g | Fiber: 1.7g | Cholesterol: 0mg | Sugar: 8.3g | Sodium: 2959mg

10.11 Sweet and Sour Dip

Preparation Time: 15 minutes | Cooking Time: 0 minutes | Servings: 15

Ingredients
- Rice Wine - 1 tbsp
- Sesame Oil - 1 tbsp
- Ginger – ½ tsp
- Garlic - 1 clove
- Honey - 1 tsp
- Chili Pepper – ½ tsp
- Scallions - for garnish
- Soy Sauce - 2 tbsp

Preparation
1. Mix ginger and garlic and put them in a bowl.
2. Add all Ingredients and top with chopped scallions.
3. Ready to serve.

Nutritional Facts
Calories: 157 | Carbohydrates: 10.9g | Protein: 2.5g | Fat: 10.3g | Fiber: 1.1g | Cholesterol: 0mg | Sugar: 9.3g | Sodium: 2499mg

10.12 Avocado Fish Sauce

Preparation Time: 25 minutes | Cooking Time: 0 minutes | Servings: 15

Ingredients
- Tamari - 2 tbsp
- Sesame Oil - ½ tsp
- Avocado Mayo - ½ cup
- Ginger (Grounded) - ½ tsp
- Fish Sauce - 1 tsp
- Lemon Juice - 3tsp
- Red Chili Flakes - ½ tsp
- Black Pepper - ½ tsp

Preparation
1. Whisk all above items and stir them evenly.
2. Dish out with seafood and fish dumplings.

Nutritional Facts
Calories: 378 | Carbohydrates: 31.3g | Protein: 7.5g | Fat: 19g | Fiber: 7.5g | Cholesterol: 0mg | Sugar: 31g | Sodium: 2397mg

11 CONCLUSION

This cookbook has a collection of 150 recipes that contain clear and concise information for different types of food lovers. It accommodates vegetarian, vegan, beef, pork, seafood, poultry and sweet dumpling recipes. Various dipping sauce recipes have also been incorporated in this cookbook. This manual is not only easy to use but everyone will end up being a dumpling lover.

The main characteristics of this cookbook are listed below

- Handy
- Practically Convenient
- Affordable Recipes
- Go to Dumpling Meals
- Detailed Serving Size Guide
- Nutritional Content of Each Food Item Used
- Standard Metrics Conversions
- No Special Ingredients
- Aversion of Expensive Items,

And most importantly, each recipe in this book is designed to be nutritionally healthy and appropriate, keeping in mind the prevalence of most common diseases such as Diabetes, Hypertension, and Hypercholesterolemia. This book can also be used by pregnant females since it contains less salt and oils, has a calorie deficit and is dense in nutrients. Now, every individual can enjoy dumplings while keeping track of serving sizes, calories, and body requirements.

BONUS: Scanning the following QR code will take you to a web page where you can access 7 fantastic bonuses after leaving your email and an honest review of my book on Amazon: five online courses about sushi making and 2 mobile apps with other sushi recipes.

Link: https://dl.bookfunnel.com/sw3ag9ysyt

Printed in Great Britain
by Amazon